BARRA

Helen McGregor & John Cooper

CANONGATE

First published in 1984
by Canongate Publishing Limited
17 Jeffrey Street, Edinburgh

Revised edition published in 1987

British Library Cataloguing in Publication Data
McGregor, Helen
Barra—2nd Edition
I. Barra—Description and travel
I. Title   II. Cooper, John, 1939–
914.11′4   DA 880.B3
ISBN 0 86241 165 3   September 1987

Designed by Jennifer Law
Printed and bound by BAS Printers Limited, Over Wallop, Hampshire

Acknowledgements

My grateful acknowledgement and thanks are extended to Father Angus J. MacQueen for his kindness in directing my thoughts on Catholic Barra. For their care and enthusiasm in handling the manuscript, my thanks to Laura Cooper, Caroline Pearson and Elizabeth Sherriff. To Patricia Loy of the Scottish Department, Central Library, Edinburgh for her cheerful help; to Doctor Barbara Horne of Register House, Edinburgh, Doctor J. Morton Boyd, Nature Conservancy, Scotland, Doctor Peacock of the Institute of Geological Sciences and John MacInnes of the School of Scottish Studies for help with Gaelic and Norse. My thanks are due to them all. Last but certainly not least, my gratitude and thanks to my husband Cecil for his practical support and encouragement.

Helen McGregor

All of the extracts of poetry included derive directly from the *Carmina Gadelica*, a work in four volumes of Gaelic scholarship of hymns and incantations collected orally by Dr. Alexander Carmichael. Grateful acknowledgement is given to the Scottish Academic Press Ltd for their permission for this use.

Bibliography

Borstram, C. H. J., Campbell, J. L., MacKenzie, Sir Compton, editors, *The Book of Barra*, Edinburgh, 1936

Buchan, Peter, *Ancient Scottish Tales*, Peterhead, 1908

Buchanan, Dr. D. F., F.R.S.E., *Reflections on the Isle of Barra*, London, 1942

Campbell, John F. of Islay, *Popular Tales of the Western Highlands*, Edmonston and Douglas, Edinburgh, 1862

Carmichael, Dr. Alexander, *Carmina Gadelica*, vols, I, II, III, IV, Scottish Academic Press, 1971

Douglas, Sir George, *Scottish Fairy and Folk Tales*, London, 1936

Kirkwood, Rev. Jas., *Collection of Highland Rites and Customs*, (1650–1709), edit. by J. L. Campbell, Folklore Society, Cambridge, 1975

Macdonald, Colin, *Echoes of the Glen*, Moray Press, London and Edinburgh, 1936

MacGregor, A. A., *The Peat Fire Flame*, Moray Press, Edinburgh and London, 1937

MacGregor, A. A., *The Enchanted Isles*, Michael Joseph, London, 1967

MacGregor, Alexander, *Highland Superstitions*, Stirling, 1922

MacKenzie, Donald, *Wonder Tales from Scottish Myths and Legends*, Blackie, 1917

MacLagan, Dr. R. C., *The Evil Eye in the Western Highlands*, London, 1902

MacLeod, Dr. Kenneth, *The Road to the Isles*, Edinburgh, 1927

MacNeill, Robert Lister, *Clan MacNeill*, Edinburgh and New York, 1923

MacPherson, John ('the Coddy'), *Tales from Barra*, edited by J. L. Campbell, Edinburgh, 1960

Martin, Martin, *Barra in 1695*, from *A Description of the Western Isles*, Edinburgh, 1703

Murray, W. H., *The Hebrides*, London, 1966

Napier Commission Report, *Evidence given by the Barra Clergy*, London, 1892

Nature Conservancy Council, *The Natural Environment of the Outer Hebrides*, edit. by Dr. Morton Boyd, Royal Society, Edinburgh, 1979

Polson, A., F.S.A. Scot., *Our Highland Folklore Heritage*, Northern Chronicle Office, Inverness, 1926

Scott-Moncrieff, George, *The Mirror and the Cross*, Catholic Book Club, London, 1960

Stewart, W. Grant, *Popular Superstitions and Festive Amusements of the Highlands of Scotland*, Edinburgh, 1823

Sutherland, Douglas, *Behold the Hebrides*, London, 1968

THE SUN

From John MacNeill, cottar, Buaile nam Bodach, Barra

Hail to thee, thou sun of the seasons,
    As thou traversest the skies aloft;
Thy steps are strong on the wing of the heavens,
    Thou art the glorious mother of the stars.

Thou liest down in the destructive ocean
    Without impairment and without fear;
Thou risest up on the peaceful wave-crest
    Like a queenly maiden in bloom.

BARRA

The Outer Hebrides form a long chain of islands which protect the north west of Scotland from the fury of the Atlantic ocean. The Barra Isles, the most southerly and westerly group, consist of about twenty islands and are uninhabited except for Vatersay and Barra, although a few of the larger islands are used for grazing. Their names, Vatersay, Sandray, Pabbay, Mingulay and Berneray sing like the *clarsach*, the little harp of twenty-eight strings. Their surround-ing seas are the domain of seals, basking sharks, dolphins, porpoises, sea otters and killer whales.

The pendant-shaped island of Barra has an area of approximately thirty-five square miles. There is a circular single track road about fourteen miles long. A four-mile branch road from North Bay, with two short spurs leading to clachans, bypasses the Traigh Mhor — now Barra's unique cockle-strand airfield — which it used to cross at low tide. The road winds north to Eoligarry and Kilbar chapel, and past a formidable boulder beach to the furthermost cottage on the north of the island.

The centre of Barra is mountainous, rising to 1,260 feet at the summit of Heaval. The view from the spine of the island is breathtaking. On a clear day looking west to the edge of the Atlantic shelf, the thousand-foot cliffs of St. Kilda are visible; these are the remains of a vast four-mile wide volcanic crater.

The rock formation of the Outer Hebrides is particularly interesting being mainly Lewisian gneiss, dating as far back as 2,800 million years, the oldest in Britain. Some of Barra's coastline is jagged and precipitous, and it is deeply indented, especially to the north east. The cliffs and caves on exposed parts of the west coast are broken by magnificent beaches of dazzling white sand, pounded incessantly by seas of luminous greens and purple. The narrow isthmus on the road to the Eoligarry peninsula has a line of sand dunes which are constantly moved by the winter gales despite the frantic planting of marram grass.

The sea birds are a varied population of puffins, razor-bills, guillemots, shags and occasionally the great northern diver. Most of these breed and nest on the ledges of the great cliffs of Berneray and Mingulay below which are long sea galleries and arcades. The highest cliff, measuring eight hundred feet, is at Aonaig on Mingulay and has a perpendicular face. Centuries ago the MacNeills named it Biolacraig, adopted the precipice as part of their crest and used the name as their rallying cry. The shore line is populated by a large range of waders such as ringed plovers and pipits, while a variety of small birds like sanderlings come and go with their seasons.

It is believed that the name Barra has belonged to the island since its earliest habitation and may well

have been in use when the Celts arrived around 1,000 BC. The Hebrides have been inhabited by five civilisations during the last 6,500 years – the Mesolithic or Middle Stone Age, and the Iron, Bronze, Viking and Celtic Ages.

The name of Barra could have come into being and been used by any of the people of these civilisations. This being accepted, the supposition that the island is named after Finnbar, Bishop of Cork, who was one of Saint Columba's missionaries in the sixth and seventh centuries, seems rather improbable. It would be easy to accept Barra as the island of this much-loved and venerated early Celtic saint (not forgetting Saint Brendan who didn't stay long) but there is evidence which suggests otherwise. One theory is that Finnbar may have visited the island and left a missionary to represent himself called *gille Barra*, meaning 'lad or servant of Barra'. It appears to have existed as a Christian name at that time, although it is now no longer in use. Another theory is that the saint never visited Barra but that only his name was used, as a mark of honour.

The vast majority of place-names in and around Barra and the Hebrides are a mixture, fairly equally divided, of the Gaelic and Norwegian languages. It has been suggested that the ancient spelling of the name as *Barray* might derive from its particular situation or bearing, because the Norse word for island includes the letters *Ay* or *I*, while *Barr* in Gaelic means a point or top. Thus Barray formed a point or top island towards the south end of the chain of the Outer Hebrides – a navigational guide for the longships sailing from Norway.

Later, the religion brought to Iona was carried to and deeply rooted in Barra by Saint Brendan (484–558 AD). The adventurous navigator-evangelist built a tiny chapel near Borve where he lived for a short time before sailing off into the Atlantic to visit St. Kilda, Greenland and some say even far-away America. It is probable that Saint Finnbar (550–623 AD) was close behind him, if not with him. Whichever way Barra received its name, Finnbar is certainly its titular Saint; it is believed that he lived where he founded *Chille Bharra* (The Church of St. Barr) at Kilbar in Eoligarry, the most northerly part of the island. He was greatly beloved by the people, ninety percent of whom became Roman Catholics. The islanders, out of love, named the twenty-fifth of September as a special day for Saint Barr.

There are no rivers on Barra, but a few streams drain some of the bog land in the centre of the island, in particular one on the west coast near Borve and another near Ersary on the east coast. Further north a burn tumbles from the reservoir of Loch an Duin past the site of an old water mill and down a steep wooded glen to North Bay. Loch St. Clair, situated below Ben Tangaval, has a small well, known as St. Columba's, and there are several smaller lochs scattered around the island.

The population is now over 1,200 with Castlebay the main residential area, but there are many smaller settlements, which include Northbay, Eoligarry and Craigston – Borve, Allasdale, Brevig, Cleat and Nask to name but a few.

Today only a small part of the island is intensively cultivated, but in the past the rich alluvial valley shared by Borve and Craigstone and also the fertile Eoligarry area, would have been growing bere or six-row barley and later on oats of the black, sandy or potato variety, and probably rye and spelt wheat. These would have been ground at the water mill below Loch an Duin. There was also much cultivation on the steeper slopes of the island; evidence of 'lazy beds', where potatoes were grown, is seen in

many areas of the machair to the west of Borve and on Greian Head. The 'lazy beds' can be recognised by the lines, about five feet apart, running down the hillside. The potatoes were laid on the grass and were covered by the upturned turves taken from the area between the beds. This was deepened to form the lines of drainage ditches, the earth from which covered the beds.

In the centre of the island is wild moorland with fescue agrostis type grass and sedge. Ling and bell heather also grow and occasionally the rare whites are to be found. There are very few trees on Barra; a small group in the shelter of Heaval above Brevig and in the gulley down to Northbay, with a few including a monkey-puzzle at the head of Bay Hulavagh. Some say that the norsemen burnt all the island's forests so that the enemy would more easily be seen.

Barra has a large and varied population of birds, many of whom live inland and are of the small finch and skylark variety. Wheatears, wagtails, larks and twites are much in evidence, while sightings of siskins, blackcaps and redpolls are more rare. Flitting amongst the fragrant machair and in the immensity of the sky, the charm and clarity of their song is intensified by the silence. There are red shanks and snipe in the marshy places and the cuckoo's song can be heard in the glens. In the past, birds of prey were plentiful although they are rarely seen today.

One of the most exciting things about arriving in Barra is the realisation that only the incomers speak English, which is considered a second language. The first language of the islanders is still Gaelic, the Barra dialect being of a particularly soft and pleasing intonation. Having survived the discouragement of their language in the eighteenth and nineteenth centuries, the problem now lies in constructing it around present-day English with its explosive vocabulary, expansion of technical terms, and the new concepts of the past fifty years.

In May, the season of wild flowers transforms Barra with acres of fragrant loveliness, reputed to flavour with nectar the milk from the cows. Extravagant drifts of blue scilla or squill delight the eye on Greian Head where the grazing is scattered with eyebright, wild geranium and celandine. Thousands of wild orchids from creamy white to purple, and some strains of a rare red Hebridean colour, jostle for space with lousewort, selfheal and tormentil in the damp places. Amongst the flowers to be found on the rock edges are thyme, roseroot, sea-pinks and mountain everlasting. In the boggy ground there are bright yellow marsh marigolds and the stately flag iris. Sundew and purple-flowered butterwort trap insects and midges for their nourishment. To walk on the acres of fragrant primroses at Eoligarry is the stuff of dreams.

The air, freed from the contamination of the mainland, is pure and deeply healing, while the sea in all its moods has a strong influence on the lives of

the people. The sense of isolation and space is accentuated by the changing light which illuminates the colours and creates a memorable picture of the whole island.

All the beauty of the Hebrides can be found concentrated within the small space of Barra. The warm dry scent of sweet vernal grass in the sheltered glens, the rustle of the marram on the machair, the soft breath of grazing beast, the startled ewe, the eerie song of a seal, the stirring of the sand amongst the shingle and the beat of wings, dark against the evening sky, are all part of the magic.

RELIGION

The Druids were a late product of the pagan world and appear to have been a combination of priest and philosopher. There is no definite evidence that establishes their presence at any time in Barra, but their pagan influence is evident in the superstitions and folklore.

The Gaelic word for 'very wise' is *druid* and frequently Saint Columba spoke of Christ as 'His Druid' and even 'His Arch Druid'. Over the centuries Christians have absorbed pagan symbols and rituals.

The early Celts had no priesthood and no temple worship. The Gods had to be propitiated but were not idealised. The Celts were more in favour of hero worship and less partial to virtue than others. They were inured to facing the inhospitable world in the

mass with all its unconquered immensities, and it is little wonder that they personified the elemental forces as deities and invoked them as such.

The Columban Tradition of the sixth or seventh centuries was founded by Saint Patrick about 447 AD and Germanus was created its first Bishop. The See of the Isles became vacant at the end of the fourteenth century and remained so for 325 years. The See of Argyll was created as a detachment from Dunkeld in 1200, and it was vacant for more than 300 years. James Hamilton was appointed to this See in 1553 but it is probable that he was never consecrated. Since 1978 the combined Sees have been jointly administered as the See of Argyll and the Isles.

During the Reformation of the Church in the sixteenth century, Barra was one of the remote places which escaped the excessive zeal of the militant clergy. Likewise Barra's own Catholic church perhaps did not have as much contact with the inhabitants as it had in its latter years. This is why many old and strange customs survived. A hundred years passed without any regular ministration until in the year 1652 Father Duggan, a Catholic priest from Limerick, set off to the Isles at the invitation of Glengarry of Uist and apparently in disguise. He wrote to Saint Vincent de Paul, 'In these islands and in the whole of the Highlands of Scotland there are no priests except my companions and myself. We have accepted no recompense from the people for services rendered. I have to employ two men; one helps me to row when I travel from island to island, and carries my Mass-box and scanty luggage, for sometimes before Mass I have to travel four or five leagues on foot over wretched roads. The other man helps me to teach the *Pater, Ave* and *Credo* and serves my Mass, for I have nobody else capable of doing so. . . . We take only one meal a day, consisting of barley or oaten bread with some cheese or salt butter. Sometimes we spend whole days without a meal . . . As for meat, we hardly ever eat it. . . . If we wished to buy some meat . . . we could not get small quantities, for there is no butcher in the islands. We should have to purchase a cow or a sheep and this we cannot do, owing to our continual journeys to administer Baptism and the other Sacraments.'

In every kind of weather they went where they knew they were needed, answering the call, sleeping rough or on a hard-packed earth floor, walking for miles through dark and storm, arriving at the shore to sit behind a rock; seeking shelter for hours awaiting the arrival of a boat to carry them to administer a blessing and give comfort and absolution to the sick and dying.

Father Duggan must have been a hardy and dedicated man, living on poor food and being rowed around the Isles with many arduous duties. Initially, he found the people superstitious and difficult until he arrived in Barra – at the invitation of the MacNeill. He was surprised to find so many people unmarried but soon realised that this situation was caused by the absence of any priest; he also noticed that the people obtained great satisfaction from the ceremonial use of Holy Water.

Later, Father Duggan wrote; 'At the beginning of spring I landed upon another island, named Barra, where I found a people so devout and anxious to learn that I was astonished. It is enough to teach one child in each village the *Pater, Ave* and *Credo*; in two days the whole village know them – children and adults.'

It is obvious that he regarded Barra with particular affection, which fact was recognised by the islanders who named a pass over the hills, *Bealach A'Ghugain* (Pass of Duggan) to commemorate his devoted

wanderings nearly three centuries ago. During the five years of his ministry in Barra the Catholic faith was so well established that any Protestant minister who visited made no headway.

It was when the persecution by Oliver Cromwell was at its height that Father Duggan prepared to set off on a 'dangerous mission'. He became ill and died in May 1657. The remoteness of Barra saved it from the fury of the rest of Protestant Scotland, which continued for over a hundred years. With great difficulty a few priests from Ireland, wisely chosen as Gaelic speakers, continued to minister to the people.

In a 'Report to the Sacred Congregation' in 1669 Dr Winston said; 'The Highlanders are of excellent disposition, quick of intellect, taking a special delight in the pursuit of Knowledge. They are desirous of novelties and have an unbounded passion for ingenious inventions. No greater favour can be conferred upon them than to educate their children and render them suited to become priests or ecclesiastics. Their untiring constancy in all matters is truly surprising and is admitted and extolled even by their enemies, particularly in regard of religion, which they continue to profess as much as the severity of the persecution and the total want of priests permit.'

A Catholic school was founded in Barra in 1675

with another at Glengarry, on the mainland; they were the only two in all Scotland. After much propaganda from the Cardinals insisting that all Roman Catholic children must be sent to these schools, Dr. Winston protested that Catholic parents would as soon send their children to Jamaica – as to Barra!

Two years later Father Francis Macdonel mentions the number of Catholics on the island as being about 1,000 including the Laird.

At this time the unpopular Union of the Crowns was being promoted and the authorities, with memories of Montrose's successful campaign using Irish mercenaries, were on the look-out for any Irish who might be preparing the way for the French. It was recommended that no Irish missionaries should be sent but that local Gaelic speakers be recruited and trained.

Seven years later William Leslie, on a visit with Munro, writes of the determination of the Barramen to have their own resident priest. They threatened forcibly to detain their priest on the island and even to burn their boats, unless a solemn promise was made to grant their wishes.

It was impossible for any Catholic to hold land, and this may have been the reason why the MacNeills became Protestants. Catholic tenants were discouraged, but in no case was there any persecution such as was initiated by Macdonald of Boisdale in South Uist. By 1840 the sixty Protestant incomers who came to Barra in 1813 had increased to 380.

Today there are four Catholic churches and one Protestant. The Venerable Church of St. Brendan at Craigstone is a replacement of an old church on the same site, and all the islanders lent a helping hand in the rebuilding. Timber washed up on the beaches was collected as there is no wood on the island, and stone was brought from wherever it could be obtained, from as far away as Sandray. Cockleshells from Eoligarry sands were conveyed by pannier on ponies for incineration into lime for the building. In the days of the very early church at Craigston there was one priest, and much faith and pastoral duties operated from the one centre there. Later, from about 1626 to 1640, Franciscan missionaries worked on Barra. At Castlebay, the Church of our Lady Star of the Sea was built by appeal and opened on Christmas day, 1889.

A modern statue of Saint Barr by Margaret Somerville stands on a small islet facing the Northbay church, which, like St. Vincent's at Eoligarry, is comparatively new. The Protestant church was built inland north of Allasdale with a large, beautifully situated manse overlooking Seal Bay.

The islanders are a strong and simple people, whose spirits in the dim past were bolstered by charms and spells to counteract unpredictable and fearful dangers. They were deeply aware of everyday perils and the protective shield of God was very real. The invoking of good spirits through prayer was their strong aid. The wildness of their world was harnessed and subjected to God who was seen clearly as master of the elements, of humanity and of the spirit. God was very real, infinite, loving and within, *de nan dul* (the living God of life and God of all).

Religion, language and culture have always been part of the tapestry and saga of the Barra Islands. Although the people had a feeling of family unity arising from an often mythical kinship with their laird or chief, it was the priest who was the custodian of their tradition. This was handed down by word of mouth. In the Catholic islands the fiddles were never burnt on the bonfire as the Reformation scarcely touched them, and as a result the sanctuary lamps were never extinguished.

THE RED-STALK

Pluck will I the little red-stalk of surety,
The lint the lovely Bride drew through her palm,
For success of health, for success of friendship,
    For success of joyousness,
For overcoming of evil mind, for overcoming of evil eye,
    For overcoming of bewitchment,
For overcoming of evil deed, for overcoming of evil conduct,
    For overcoming of malediction,
For overcoming of evil news, for overcoming of evil words,
    For success of blissfulness—
    For success of blissfulness.

AN DEARG CHASACHAN

Buainidh mi an dearg⁄chasachan aic,
An lion a bhuain Bride mhin tromh glaic,
Air buaidh shlainte, air buaidh chairdeas
    Air buaidh thoileachais,
Air buaidh droch run, air buaidh droch shul,
    Air buaidh chronachais.
Air buaidh droch bheud, air buaidh droch bheus,
    Air buaidh ghonachais,
Air buaidh droch sgeul, air buaidh droch bheul,
    Air buaidh shonachais—
    Air buaidh shonachais.

HISTORY

The first people who inhabited the Outer Hebrides have long been forgotten and little remains of their existence but some burial mounds and stones.

There is evidence of there being an early Celtic presence on the islands in about 1,000 BC. The Norse invasion was later still, about 800 AD. Although the Vikings came to raid and plunder, they finally settled on the islands and colonised them. After a very long period, which is well documented, the overlordship of Norway was finally surrendered, and these islands were returned to Scotland by treaty after the Battle of Largs in 1266.

When peace returned, the colourful threads of an almost classless society were drawn together under the MacDonalds who were then Lords of the Isles. It was a happy and prosperous time which lasted for 200 years, free from the evils of feudalism.

However, the various Scots kings were always anxious and uncomfortable when they realised how strongly independent the islands were, as by this time the Lords of the Isles were making their own laws and were under their own jurisdiction. The Hebrides were too inaccessible for obedience to be enforced, and when the Royal Authority was repeatedly and openly flouted it was the last straw. James IV ordered that John Donald, the fourth Lord of the Isles, was to be arrested, and he was brought to trial in 1493. The lands and titles of MacDonald were declared forfeit to the Crown.

This resulted in over a hundred years of anarchy. Chief fought against chief and clan against clan. The lands were ravaged and people were scandalised by the frightful, lawless conditions which prevailed on the islands until King James VI succeeded in 1603.

He captured most of the chiefs by the ruse of inviting them to a parley aboard his flagship *Moon* — which then sailed for Edinburgh. The chiefs were only released upon the condition that they agreed to ratify the statutes drawn up by Andrew Knox, Bishop of the Isles.

These were the nine Statutes of Iona (*Ikolmkill*), which more or less succeeded in their object:

1. They should accept the discipline of the Reformed Church and maintain the clergy and the churches.
2. They should establish inns to relieve the people of burdensome hospitality.
3. They should support their own households out of their own resources and not by taxing tenants, and allow no man to live on the isles without a trade or personal income.
4. *Sorners*, (men who lived by quartering themselves free on defenceless families) should be punished as thieves.
5. Excessive drinking should be curbed. Men might brew drink for their own use but not import it.
6. Every man having sixty or more cattle must send his son to a lowland school.
7. The use of firearms was to be forbidden.
8. Bards glorifying war should be discouraged as idlers.
9. Previous acts which had been ignored should not be enforced.

The feuding between the clans diminished to a large extent and the clan system was nearly at an end when the death blow was struck at the Battle of Culloden in 1745. Barra had its share of Redcoats during the aftermath of this disastrous rebellion, when the island held French money and stored supplies.

It was a Barraman, Duncan Cameron, who was responsible for our knowledge of the early days of the rising. He was on board the French ship, *Du Teillay* when they first sighted Barra Head. He landed on Barra and met MacNeill's piper who piloted the ship to Eriskay, where the Prince landed. During the search for the Prince after Culloden, many famous English naval officers gained their experience trying to seal off the Minch at each end. Because of their shallow draught, several of the tiny French ships trying to rescue the Prince managed to evade the net by navigating the narrow sounds. The final attempt was successful and the Pretender slipped through the cordon. MacNeill had not committed himself or his clansmen to the Stuart cause but this did not prevent his arrest by the notorious and brutal Captain

Ferguson, who treated him most cruelly. MacNeill survived imprisonment in the English hulks and was released in 1747.

After 1745, the clansmen were finally disarmed and the wearing of tartan forbidden. The Chiefs lost jurisdiction and became landlords, the clansmen becoming tenants, a system existing to the present day.

The events which followed the ill-fated rebellion destroyed Gaeldom as a whole, although only a small minority of clans had participated in it. Every device was employed to abolish all distinction between Island, Highland and Lowland Scots, and the so-called evictions of the mid-nineteenth century changed the scene for ever.

At the end of the Napoleonic Wars in 1815 an extensive report was written by John MacCulloch, a well known geologist and Doctor of Medicine. His writings were thorough and descriptive but alas did nothing to mitigate the poverty of the islanders. His way of thinking was adopted by the landowners and led to the break-up of the small crofts, followed by extensive emigration encouraged and often forced by the landowner. The inefficiency of the small crofter was understandable, being caused by the persecution after the '45, the labour demands of his laird, his lack of any security of tenure and the fact that he might actually be penalised for any improvements which he may have made.

The letters from the MacNeill to the Revd. Angus MacDonald at the time show that there was much discontent. While being reasonably sympathetic the letters show that any dissatisfied tenants would soon find themselves dispossessed. At the start of the eighteenth century MacNeill was still a vassal of Mac-Donald of Sleat, but apart from having to supply the usual able men and a hawk, the annual rent was just over three pounds.

During the latter years of General MacNeill's ownership of the islands he strove desperately to avoid bankruptcy. He raised rents and built a kelp factory but finally sold the island in 1839 to a speculator, who resold it to Colonel Gordon of Cluny within a year for £38,000 – at a loss of £4,000.

In 1840 an excellent and full report on the islands was written by the Revd Alexander Nicolson. It contained much sound advice which unfortunately was ignored for over fifty years. Things got worse and the potato famine of 1845–46 was a terrible disaster. Times were very difficult indeed. A collection of letters written by Donald MacLeod in 1851 to the Edinburgh Weekly Chronicle give a tragic account of the state of Barra, drawing attention to some of the dreadful results of what became known as 'The Evictions'.

Over 1,000 people from the island were transported to Canada. At this time discontent in the Highlands and islands became of such serious dimensions that the Crofters Commission was set up to take evidence and make recommendations. It is obvious that the small crofters and the larger farmers and landowners had drifted very far apart.

One of the principal witnesses for the islanders, Michael Buchanan, did not himself rent a croft and could therefore not be discriminated against. He presented an excellent case and spoke well. His main grievance was not against the owner, Lady Gordon Cathcart, who was the daughter of Colonel Gordon Cluny, but against the main tenant farmer Dr. McGillivary of Eoligarry and the factor Ronald Mac-Donald. The factor tried to brand Buchanan as a work-shy agitator, as many of his complaints went back several decades. Both sides were given a very fair hearing although exaggeration may have taken place in some of the statements. The evidence taken

from the clergy on Barra shows how close they were to the people, an involvement which continues to this day. The Commission also received an Article describing the agricultural customs of the time from Alexander Carmichael, best known for his 'Carmina Gadelica' the famous anthology of poetry in Gaelic. He spoke highly of Lt. General MacNeill and Dr. McGillivary. Although they had much to their credit Carmichael was obviously unaware of some of the threats and dictatorial methods to which the crofters were subjected. Three years later, the Crofter's Holdings (Scotland) Act was passed, which has been described as the Magna Carta of the Highlands. The Crofters Commission eventually became the Land Court.

From then on the pendulum swung the other way. Barra and Vatersay were still not without violent troubles, especially after World War I — but today the large farmers are no more.

Eoligarry is owned by the Department of Agriculture and divided into small-holdings which are let to the crofters, while the other half of Barra has been repossessed by the MacNeill.

Probably the most prosperous times were immediately before the First World War when there was a herring boom and vast quantities were exported, but when the heroes returned from the services they were soon to be faced with the depression of the 1920s.

The failure of the inshore herring industry was of course a disaster but it is hoped that the return of business to Barra in the form of a fish factory will bring some new prosperity to the island.

RUIN

Labhram gach la a reir do cheartais,
Gach la taisbim do smachd, a Dhe;
Labhram gach la a reir do reachd-sa,
Gach la is oidhche bithim toigh riut fein.

Gach la cunntam fath do throcair,
Toirim gach la dha do nosda speis;
Gach la tionnsgam fein dhut oran,
Teillim gach la do ghloir, a Dhe.

Beirim gach la gaol dhut, Iosa,
Gach oidhche nithim da reir;
Gach la 's oidhche, duar is soillse,
Luaidhim do chaoibhneas dhomh, a Dhe.

DESIRES

May I speak each day according to Thy justice,
Each day may I show Thy chastening, O God;
May I speak each day according to Thy wisdom,
Each day and night may I be at peace with Thee.

Each day may I count the causes of Thy mercy,
May I each day give heed to Thy laws;
Each day may I compose to Thee a song,
May I harp each day Thy praise, O God.

May I each day give love to Thee, Jesu,
Each night may I do the same;
Each day and night, dark and light,
May I laud Thy goodness to me, O God.

Many clans are connected with the Barra isles, MacDonald, Campbell, MacNeill and MacKinnon to name but a few. However it is the MacNeills who are immediately associated with Barra and known to be one of the oldest amongst Hebridean dynasties.

There is no positive proof that the MacNeills spring from Niall of the Nine Hostages who ruled at Tara in Ireland during the fourth century. It is reasonable to believe that his descendant Niall came to Barra in about 1030 and married a daughter of the Norwegian King, although some say that the clan spring from Norse origin and that the name could have been Neilsson. However – the traditional clan lands of the MacNeills are the Barra isles.

In 1427 when the MacDonalds were Lords of the Isles they gave a charter of Barra to Gilleonan, son of Roderick son of Murdo son of Niall. Reckoned from the Niall, just mentioned, the last male chief of this *direct* line was General Roderick MacNeill of Barra, who died in 1863.

It is thought that the ancient MacNeill stronghold of Kishmul Castle, which is built on a rocky islet a hundred yards offshore, dates from the thirteenth century, but in all probability a curtain wall existed on the site at an earlier time. It has one of the best natural harbours in the Hebrides and the first sight of it is startling as it appears to rise dramatically, straight out of the sea. Much has been written about the MacNeills, and Kishmul's famous galley, and it believed that they owned all of Barra for centuries prior to building the castle.

In 1695 Martin Martin wrote: 'The little island Kismul lies about a quarter of a mile from the south of the isle. It is the seat of the MacNeills of Barray; there is a stone wall round it two storeys high, reaching the sea, and within the wall there is an old tower and a hall, with other houses about it. There is a little magazine [a Norse weapon store] in the tower, to which no stranger has access.'

The legendary galley was berthed alongside on a sloping beach with the galley crewhouse nearby. This was a twostorey building constructed *outside* the castle and the crewmen were expected to fight in defence, if Kishmul came under surprise attack. Reading the tales, it would appear that it was prestigious to have been a crewman on Kishmul's galley, as they most surely were a handpicked, highly trained force. Some say that they may have been slaves or prisoners under threat of dire atrocities and death, but this theory does not match the MacNeill's attitude towards his galley. It was kept ready for instant action in defence of the territory, to intercept or raid an enemy, or to rescue a king; Robert the Bruce owed his life to its prodigious speed when his retreat was cut off after a mainland battle.

Kishmul also had a fish trap in a catchment basin and, amazingly, two artesian wells. At one stage in its history a floor was placed across the entire Great Hall at a height of 7 feet, thereby doubling its capacity for sleeping fighting men, or women and children coming to the castle for shelter in times of distress. Martin Martin wrote; 'When any of the tenants are so far advanced in years that they are incapable to till the ground, MacNeill takes such old men into his own family, and maintains them all their lives after. . . . If a tenant's wife bore twins the Chief had to take one of them and bring it up with his own family.' They all slept on the ground strewing bracken or heather on the floor with roots downward, which gave passable comfort, with animal skins for covering. An account given in 1582 relates the simplicity of their food, clothing and domestic life. Hunting and fishing supplied food and the flesh was boiled with water inside the paunch or skin of the animal,

while sometimes they ate the flesh raw, merely squeezing out the blood. They drank the juice of the boiled flesh and sometimes a mixture of fluids, but mostly quenched their thirst with water. A kind of bread was made of oats and barley, although 'spelt' wheat was mentioned, the only grain cultivated in the region; a small meal was eaten in the morning and frequently they remained without food till the evening.

The defensive armour of the MacNeill clan consisted of an iron headpiece and a coat of mail, formed of small rings, frequently reaching to the heels. Their weapons were mostly bows and arrows barbed with iron which made a nasty wound. A few carried swords and Lochaber axes. Instead of a trumpet, they used bagpipes and were exceedingly fond of music, employing harps of a peculiar kind which they delighted in adorning with silver and gems, the poorer people substituting crystals. Their songs in general celebrated brave men, their bards seldom choosing any other subject.

To the great displeasure of the MacNeill of that time a seer predicted that one day Kishmul would become the home of sea birds and otters. It was eventually abandoned in the eighteenth century after the family had built a more comfortable house at Eoligarry. Viewed through time the MacNeills appear as flamboyant, dramatic characters and men of great seamanship; lusty sea-rovers and raiders. Their splendid boats of Norse design and speed were nicknamed 'The Greyhounds of the Sea', which captured the imagination and made them greatly feared. Tales of the MacNeill are legion and packed with adventure, unbelievable feats of endurance and much humour, and like many entertaining stories they are often larger-than-life, but always enthralling.

There is a tale of ancient times when Kishmul's Galley was long overdue from a raid. As it returned across the Minch a great wind came which was so terrible that every man aboard was forced to take an oar. The people on Barra watched and prayed while the MacNeill from the castle ramparts gave orders that all the lookouts on the hills must increase their vigilance and the fiery cross be relayed with all speed around Barra. Immediately the galley was sighted the beacons were to be lit to guide her home through the rocky harbour mouth. The people pressed into the cracks and rocks of Heaval as the hurricane snatched and tore at their bodies; spindrift and saturating rain stung their eyes and lips as their gaze strove to penetrate the lashing fury. All eyes were strained into the maelstrom when in the far distance a tiny speck breasted a monstrous wave. A shout went up from the lookouts, but was instantly torn away. The great galley struggled nearer, beating against the sea that threatened to swamp her while the sharp eyes of a lookout could see men stripped of their shirts and rowing for their lives.

The MacNeill sent word to heat blankets and prepare the drink and meat that was awaiting their arrival. A huge fire was lit in the open courtyard at Kishmul and the beef hung nearby with orders that none of the crewmen must eat or drink for twelve hours after their arrival. Later, when the galley came into the shelter of the castle, the crew were so exhausted they had to be lifted out and carried, dreadfully bruised with muscles strained to breaking point. Men stood ready to massage them from head to foot with whisky and wrap them in hot blankets where they fell into a coma of oblivion. Once the crewmen had recovered there was a feast with chunks of roasted beef and beakers of whisky, no one man receiving more than another, and there was great rejoicing. They were given rest for a few days after which they

sent a message to the MacNeill to the effect that 'if he required another raid of them, they were ready to go'.

The MacNeills had a 'fine conceit' of themselves as well as a sense of humour. A tradition associated with Kishmul Castle was the proclamation from the great tower; 'Hear, O ye people, and listen all ye nations, the great MacNeill of Barra has finished his meal, the princes of the earth may now dine!'

Another story tells of how at the time of the flood Noah sent a messenger inviting the MacNeill and his Lady to join him in the Ark – to which he replied, 'We thank you, but the MacNeill has a boat of his own.'

Long ago the MacNeills went on one of their many raids to Morven, which is on the north side of Mull. The inhabitants must have got word of their intention as all the cattle were concealed and there was not a beast in sight. Although the MacNeills searched and walked all through the night, with the war galley of Kishmul following silently behind them along the Sound – nothing was found. Arriving at the dead of night opposite the holy isle of Iona they decided to cross over for a visit in the hope of some spoil in the absence of cattle. Near the sacred Abbey they found beautifully carved burial stones, which were the size of a body and of great antiquity, and as there were nine men of the MacNeill there they decided to carry one each which would equal the necessary ballast for the Galley. These they brought across the Minch to the church-yard at Kilbar, where they were laid on MacNeill graves. One stone has a huge claymore and another a smaller sword, while there are stones with a ship, a dog or horse and other animals, and one with two faces side by side. But the most outstanding one is the Kilbar stone which is the only rune-inscribed stone found in the Hebrides. Of Christian/Nordic times, there is a cross on the front with a pattern and bordered scroll while on the reverse side written vertically are the words, 'This cross has been raised in memory of Thorgeth, daughter of Steiner.'

There is a legend told of the pebbles, found on the shores of Iona, known as 'The Mermaid's Tears'. A mermaid fell in love with a saint who prayed earnestly that she might be endowed with human speech and a soul which could be saved; but she could not forgo her life at sea and when she came ashore to meet him for the last time her tears were petrified into beautiful glistening stones.

Another time the MacNeill himself was returning in his famous war galley when it was enshrouded in thick fog somewhere south of Barra Head. Having no compass they were in quite a predicament. Luckily it was calm, as the cliffs and rocks of Berneray have claimed endless victims. However, MacNeill himself took charge and as it was late in the day, he watched the direction of the sea birds as he knew they were returning to their nests. He sat in the prow of the galley peering into the fog until there was the call 'Cliffs ahead' and there, sure enough, looming throught the mist, were the towering cliffs off Barra Head. With the confidence of a great seaman he directed the crewmen, and they rowed a zigzag course through most dangerous seas across the Sound of Berneray, along the shore of Mingulay and across the Sound of Pabbay till they came to the Sound of Vatersay and thence to the safety of Kishmul.

Before the Norsemen completely took over the Hebrides, regular raids were made by them on Barra, and so great was their strength that most of the island was ravaged and occupied – except for Kishmul which held out against its besiegers. The ancient fortress was persistently blockaded in the hope of

starving the garrison into submission. Time passed, and with ever increasing hunger the garrison tightened their belts, until MacNeill's bardess, Nic Fhinn, had the clever idea of dyeing a cow's hide a different colour each day and hanging it over the battlements of Kishmul to dry, thus pretending that the defenders had an ample supply of emergency rations. The ruse worked. The Norsemen watched with incredulity the apparently endless supply of cattle being slaughtered and, wearying of their long siege, weighed anchor and sailed away to Lochlann.

The Isle of Fuday lies in the Sound of Barra between Barra and South Uist and it was here that the last of the Norwegian invaders were finally defeated in battle by the MacNeills. It was a cruel fight until the last remaining Norsemen retreated to their galley and sailed for Lochlann, never to return. After the killing the bodies were mutilated, the heads being severed and thrown into a well on Fuday which became known as 'The Well of the Heads', while the place where the battle had been fought was called 'The Bog of Blood'.

Roderick seems to have been a favourite christian name of the MacNeills as there have been no fewer than seven Chiefs of that name in the four hundred years between 1427 and 1838, with four Gilleon's and one Niall Og. It is therefore not to be wondered at that a number of the more colourful or eccentric Rodericks had nicknames. Ruari the Black (Roderick, 38th Chief of MacNeill) carried a huge battle axe and also fancied himself as a master swordsman, with many successful duels as proof. It came to his ear that Rob Roy MacGregor was making the same claim, which was not to be tolerated by the proud MacNeill. He journeyed to Loch Lomondside to challenge the MacGregor, a formidable opponent with unusually long arms, who fought with a huge claymore. It was a short fight as with one fell swipe from Rob Roy, Black Roderick had his sword arm almost severed, a great wound which took months to heal. Eventually he returned to Barra having decided not to challenge Rob Roy to further combat.

Another great character was *Ruaire an Tartair* (Roderick The Troublesome or Noisy). He is reputed to have been a famous pirate who at one time searched for Rockall believing that any inhabitants it might shelter owed allegiance to him. He committed the most outrageous acts of piracy. Thought to have plundered an English ship towards the end of Elizabeth's reign, he later declared war on England – single-handed. Although the contents of the ship were unloaded at Castlebay the crew appear to have been spared. A well-known diplomat called MacKenzie was enjoined to bring the MacNeill to justice and managed to kidnap him with the aid of strong wine. He was brought to Edinburgh where he admitted all these happenings before the Sheriff, who may have been a blood relation. MacNeill's main defence was that as looting on shore was the order of the day, looting afloat was quite legal – and that he was only avenging the death of His Majesty's mother!

The lost Barra Chronicle contained the history and genealogy of the MacNeill family, with poems in their praise; similar books were kept for all Highland chiefs of any importance, the best known being the Black and Red Books of Clanranald. There is a possibility that the Barra Chronicle is still in existence and may yet be found.

Black Ruari's oldest son was Roderick 'The Dove of the West', who became 39th Chief. His grandson, Roderick 'The Resolute', was killed while serving Wolfe at Quebec in 1759. His son, Roderick 'The Gentle', succeeded his grandfather and fought in the American War of Independence with his clansmen

at his side, while 'The General' was the 41st Chief and last of that long line.

Fulfilling the prediction of the seer, in 1795 Kishmul was ravaged by fire which destroyed the floors, roofs and the wooden warheads which crowned the parapets of the walls, and the castle was uninhabited for over a hundred years. As with so many abandoned castles and buildings of good stone, it was slowly reduced, the stones being used as ballast by ships that had left their cargo at Barra.

The MacNeills lived for almost another hundred years in their new 'seat' at Eoligarry, fulfilling the role of landed gentry rather than warrior chiefs, until 1838 when their finances were in such disarray that they were forced to sell all their possessions and move away from Barra. Roderick 'The General' had been admired by the people whom he had looked after and they did all that they could, but to no avail, in an attempt to help their Chief. He was thought of as a tall, upstanding handsome man with a fine military record.

However, like the phoenix, Kishmul was destined to rise again and become once more the seat and home of the MacNeills and the focal point of the clan. With the death of Roderick 'The General', the succession passed to a branch of the family that had emigrated to Canada. Its claim to the chiefship was established legally in 1915 when Robert Lister MacNeill matriculated arms in the court of the Lord Lyon in Edinburgh, which was re-matriculated in 1961, thereby laying to rest various disputes. Robert 'The Restorer and Architect', and 45th Chief, re-acquired the Estate of Barra and the ruins of Kishmul Castle, which was excavated in 1938. It was rebuilt and restored between 1956 and 1970, and this huge project was undertaken with local skills and the labour of Barramen, being financed by family funds, a government grant and generous contributions from MacNeills all over the world. Robert 'The Restorer' was succeeded by his son Ian Roderick 'The Professor' who, like his father, spends part of each year at Kishmul living within the legend which is part history, part prejudice and part mystery.

During the sixteenth century the first mention of Barra or the 'Bishops Isles' by Donald Munro, in his capacity as High Dean, was somewhat marred by his inability to converse freely with the islanders in their own tongue. The famous George Buchanan wrote further of the island but obviously based much of his writing on Munro. However, the well-known antiquarian Walter MacFarlane led us into the seventeenth century with Martin Martin who is best known of all. Martin was a Skye man and wrote with much feeling about his fellow Hebrideans.

An excellent description of the island was written in 1794 by the Church of Scotland minister the Revd. Edward MacQueen. He gives a clear picture of Barra, covering agriculture, fishing, wages, population and historical buildings and places. The observations on farming are interesting. A moderate farm employed five or six men, four or five maid servants and two or three boys, the wages being from fifteen shillings to two pounds per annum. An early example of profit sharing is mentioned, one seventh of the crop being divided among the men and boys. During June to August, between sowing and reaping, the servants and up to eighteen horses were occupied in 'winning' the peat, which was the only fuel. MacQueen thought that if the duty on coal was removed it would no longer be necessary to dig and cut peat and the servants could be more usefully employed on the kelp or seaweed, making compost

and building walls and enclosures. It should be noted that the many small crofters had little contact with the actual owner of the land who rented it out to tacksmen and large farmers. The tacksman collected all the rents which in many cases greatly exceeded the sum that the laird received. Since the '45 the power of the tacksmen had been on the wane and during the next century more and more of them emigrated. In so far as their intimate knowledge of people and farming methods was concerned, their going was a loss to the community.

WAY OF LIFE

The 'black houses' of the eighteenth century had many distinctive characteristics. A double wall was formed of loose undressed boulders, without mortar of any kind, the cavity being filled with peat and rubble to three-foot thickness. The ends were rounded and the roof rested on the innner wall leaving room for a man to walk round on top. The roof consisted of a skeleton of timber, generally procured from driftwood. This supported a covering of turf divots and straw. Any weather-proof material was used including heather, rushes and bracken. 'Bent grass', probably marram, was obtained in exchange for labour and was a luxury.

The walls were about five or six feet high. The roof was bound together by heather ropes with large stones attached to anchor it down. There were neither chimneys nor windows. Round holes in the walls admitted light on each side of the house, and were covered over with turf according to the direction of the wind. Sometimes there was a hole in the roof for emitting the smoke of the peat fire, which was placed on a flat stone in the middle of the bare earthen floor; otherwise the smoke found its way out by seeping through the thatch. The rafters were festooned with pendants of shining black peat reek and ash dust.

Cooking utensils were suspended from the birch rafters (brought from the mainland) above the fire, the pot and the griddle being the main implements used, and the food was either boiled or baked, until the introduction of the 'wall' fire and much later the 'stove'.

The house was divided into two main rooms with a bedroom at one end, which had to sleep the entire

family, and a warm kitchen/living room at the other. There was only one door. A centre compartment was sometimes devoted to housing the animals in winter, a cow, a horse and some hens, and there was no sanitation as we know it. Water was drawn from a nearby well or stream.

During the sixteenth century (1582) it was known that members of large families slept on a communal bed, made of milerach (dry seaweed) spread on the floor, which was considered primitive even at the time. Two hundred years later, it was written, 'They have seldom much furniture . . . sometimes not a chair to sit upon, a bed to sleep on, or bed-clothes to cover them from the severity of the night air.'

In the past the women and children of the Barra isles played a major part in the work of the crofts, especially while the men were away fishing, soldiering or working for the MacNeill. After visiting Berneray in 1695 Martin Martin wrote; 'The natives never go fishing while MacNeill and his steward are on the island lest seeing their plenty of fish, perhaps they might take occasion to raise their rents.' Harvesting the kelp or seaweed was a back-breaking task, the men gathering it from the sea and the girls carrying it back above the high-tide mark. It was then spread over long racks constructed of boulders where it dried in the wind and sunshine. *Shelties* (or Highland ponies) carried it in panniers, sleds or carts to fertilise the crops. Much later kelp became a thriving but short-lived industry, as it provided an ingredient in the making of gunpowder and soap. Peat was transported in the same way and much later – coal.

A characteristic of the Barra folk was a patient submission to inconvenience, fatigue and privations – a stoical endurance when legs and arms were pitted with ulcers and sores from too much contact with sea water from the fishing, the sea-ware and cockle gathering. Millions of cockles must have been consumed by the islanders over the centuries and in bad years when the crops failed, these molluscs became their staple diet. The people have always had the right to dig and collect as many as they wish and those who had horses brought sleds or carts to help with the job. The interesting misapprehension that the cockles were generated in the Well of Kilbar above the bay at Eoligarry, carried down and hatched out in the sea, lasted for many years and was similar to the supposed origin of the Barnacle Geese.

Carrageen, a fine seaweed, was also gathered from the rocks at very low tide. After washing and bleaching in the sun it was boiled with milk to make a thick pudding. When salt was scarce, fine seaweed was burnt and mixed with the cheese to preserve it. Another plentiful source of food were the wild fowl nesting on the cliffs of the Barra isles, while oil for the lamps was obtained from the fulmars. It was also obtained from the liver of fish. Wicks, called *ruffies*, were made from the pith of bullrushes or rag soaked in tallow fat which dried hard and burnt slowly. Tallow was also poured into receptacles, sometimes a sheep's gullet, and a wick was added. Candles were made from the roots of fir trees. The flesh of the large sea-birds was sometimes buried in the sand to be salted and tenderised by the sea while their eggs were considered a delicacy.

Strange things were found in the sea and after a great storm the thundering Atlantic surf would spew up a curious assortment of objects, the most common flotsam being driftwood from wrecks, a highly prized commodity which was gathered carefully.

Nearby, across the Sound of Barra, the women on the island of Eriskay became renowned for knitting a distinctive pattern into their work which represented the fundamentals of everyday life. The jerseys

were mainly of one colour and the design was imaginative and unusual as it incorporated their folklore in the work. The garment was divided around the chest with a band of criss-cross design called 'the fish nets', on either side of which was 'poor man's gold' where the stitches were done in tight moss stitch – impossible to count. Above this the upper yoke was in vertical bands divided by narrow strips called 'the sand'. At the outside shoulder were the 'marriage lines' including the 'ups and downs' which were zig-zag lines! Next, the 'windows', which were diamonds and separated from the 'tree of life', a lop-sided diamond with a small stem, by bars of 'sand'. Next to this were the 'waves of the sea', a vertical row of chevrons finishing in the centre with the 'tree of life' and a window. Below the chest, enclosed within several vertical lines of 'sand' was a repeating design of the 'windows of life' and the 'Saint Andrew's Cross' down to hip length. Depending on the enthusiasm of the knitter the sleeves were either plain or carried the pattern finishing with the 'ups and downs' and the 'marriage lines' at the wrist. A distinctive feature were the stamped silver or metal buttons on the high neck, traditionally of Norse design, which buttoned forward on the left side, and were three or four in number.

Of special interest in the event of drowning, which was the fate of many brave men who fished the wild Atlantic, was the identification their bodies carried when washed ashore. The design of the jersey showed which island the man was from, while the buttons very often indicated the actual family to which he belonged.

The English language made little or no progress on Barra, because schools were wanting. Eventually, three were built in a triangle on Barra's fourteen-mile circular 'road' where the children marched barefoot along its rough pebble surface. The number of children and attending adults was greatly reduced during seed time and harvest and at the gathering of the potato crop when many hands were needed.

When hands and feet were blue with cold and disfigured by chilblains, the only heat in the classroom was provided by the pupils themselves who each carried a peat daily to warm the school in winter. Children too young for school were taught songs and stories by their mothers and in this way they learnt a lot about life, the tricks that fate and fortune would play upon them and the traditional roots and history of their forefathers.

The Gaelic equivalent of 'The House that Jack Built' was taught to small children as 'The infant's ladder to learning a chain of cause and effect' and was the best known of all the Gaelic nursery tales.

The children in the story are called Moorachug and Meenachug and they went to gather berries, but Moorachug soon discovered that his sister was eating all his share so he stopped picking and went to find a stick to give her a whacking.

'What's thy news today, oh Voorachai?' said the rod.

'Tis my own news, that I am seeking a rod to lay on Meenachug, and she eating my share of the fruit.'

But the stick said, 'Thou wilt not get me until thou gettest an axe that will reap me.' So off went Moorachug to find an axe.

But the axe said, 'No – not until you get a stone to smooth me.'

He reached for a stone.

'Thou wilt not get me' said the stone, 'till thou gettest water to wet me.' So Moorachug reached the water.

'What's thy news today, oh Voorachai?' said the water.

'Tis my own news that I am seeking — water to stone, stone to smooth axe — axe to reap rod to whack my sister Meenachug — and she eating my share of the berries.'

But the water said, 'No you can't have me — not until you get a deer to swim me.'

So he went and found a deer.

'You will not get me till you find a dog to run me', said the deer. 'Not till you get butter to rub on my feet,' said the dog. 'Not till you get a mouse to scrape me,' said the butter. 'Not I,' said the mouse, 'till you get a cat to hunt me.'

So Moorachug found a cat.

'You won't get me till I have some milk,' said the cat. So he reached a cow.

'No milk will I give till you get a wisp of hay from the barn gillie,' said the cow.

So he ran to the barn. 'Thou wilt not get a wisp from me,' said the barn gillie, 'till thou gettest a bonnach for me from the kneading wife.' So off he went to the kneading wife (for what was probably an oat cake or bun).

'What's thy news today, oh Voorachai?' said the kneading wife and Moorachug told her the whole tale.

'Yes,' she said, 'I will give it, but first bring me water to knead it.'

'How will I bring it? There is only one sieve,' he cried in dismay. But he took the sieve to the water.

A hoodie (crow) flew over him crying, 'Little silly, put tough brown clay and moss in it.' 'Thou art right, oh hoodie,' said the boy and he filled the sieve and carried the water to the kneading wife, and got the bonnach for the barn gillie, who gave him a wisp for the cow who gave milk for the cat. The cat began to hunt the mouse, the mouse began to scrape the butter — the butter went to the feet of the dog — the dog began to run the deer — the deer swam the water — the water began to wet the stone and the stone began to smooth the axe — the axe began to reap the rod and Moorachug took it and ran to give his sister a whacking because she was eating all his berries; but when he returned to the spot — Meenachug had *BURST!*

SAODACH A' CHRUIDH

Guma dùinte dhuibh gach sloc,
Guma sùmhail dhuibh gach cnoc,
Guma clùmhaidh dhuibh gach nochd,
   Am focharadh nam fuarbheann.

Comraig Mhoire Mhàthar dhuibh,
Comraig Bhrighde ghràidhe dhuibh,
Comraig Mhìcheil àighe dhuibh,
   Lùth is làn bhur cuallach.

Tearmad Charmaig chuimir dhuibh,
Tearmad Bhriain na luinge dhuibh,
Tearmad naoimh Mhaol Duinne dhuibh
   Am bugalach 's an crualach.

Cluanas Mhoire Mhàthar dhuibh,
Cluanas Bhrighde thàna dhuibh,
Cluanas Mhìcheil àighe dhuibh,
   An creim, an cnàmh, an cnuasachd.

DRIVING THE COWS

Closed to you be every pit,
Smooth to you be every hill,
Snug to you be every bare spot,
   Beside the cold mountains.

The sanctuary of Mary Mother be yours,
The sanctuary of Brigit the loved be yours,
The sanctuary of Michael victorious be yours,
   Active and full be you gathered home.

The protection of shapely Cormac be yours,
The protection of Brendan of the ship be yours,
The protection of Maol Duinne the saint be yours
   In marshy ground and rocky ground.

The fellowship of Mary Mother be yours,
The fellowship of Brigit of kine be yours,
The fellowship of Michael victorious be yours,
   In nibbling, in chewing, in munching.

The opening of the day began with the milking of the cow – if the folk on the croft were lucky enough to own one. Thereafter, the cow was probably tethered by a rope, which was attached to a peg in the ground. This restricted the grazing and the peg was moved daily. If the croft possessed only one sheep, it was tethered in the same way as the cow.

In early times there would be little if any spare grain, except the poorest, to feed to the beasts or hens, while the few sheep kept for their wool probably fended for themselves.

The churning or making of butter would most probably have been confined to the large herds and undertaken at regular intervals by the young women. Gutting a fish for the pot and cockle-gathering were regular tasks. Any fish bones were dried, ground up and fed to the cow (and this unknowingly supplied valuable phosphorus and calcium).

The collecting of plants such as wild parsnips, berries and lovage made a welcome addition to the diet. Plant life was a natural source of healing brews and herbs, as well as dyes for the wool. In olden times the women sat in the 'dark peat corner', where every house was furnished with a wheel and a reel; they corded and spun and had their yarn woven into cloth by a neighbouring weaver. They also did their own dyeing so that the inhabitants of each area had their leather, and the cloth of their own making.

Their ancestors wore plaids of many different colours but the majority of Barra folk preferred dark brown. However, they delighted in variegated garments, especially striped, the favourite colours being purple and blue. Archbishop Plunket, Primate of all Ireland, who was about to visit the Hebrides in 1671 wrote; 'It will be necessary for me to dress after the manner of these people, which is very different from that of every other part of the globe.' Further details of style were written by a young priest; 'They still retain the language and costume of their earliest forefathers, so that their dress is not unlike the ancient statues in Rome, loosely covered from the waist to the knee and they wear a bonnet on the head.' He was, of course, describing the belted plaid. In spite of evidence that the belted plaid had been worn, the custom did not survive the proscription of 1746.

The wool was dyed after it was spun and the interesting custom of *waulking* or shrinking the cloth took place on its return from the weaver. Two rows of six young girls sat facing each other, singing while they trod the cloth, getting faster and faster as the cloth lightened and the strong smell of urine (used to fix the dye) was released from the material.

There were different songs for the different stages of *waulking*. Starting fairly slowly, the girls got into the swing of the work, becoming more lively with a 'tightening' song. 'Stretching and clapping' songs ensured that the cloth was of even width, and were followed by the 'folding' song. Long ago they sang the 'Consecration of the Cloth' – *Coisrigea dh an adaich*. Although it had many chants and tunes it was not often heard after the nineteenth century.

The sunwise turn once, turn twice, turn thrice,
The sun to the Western Sea
Mankind to the Holy Three
In each deed for aye and aye, and in the gladnesses
The blessing of the Lord on this cloth
May heroes wear it, enjoy it, by sea, by land in
The changes of mighty waves.
One song on it, two songs, three songs
And may there be sewed to it never
But music – laughter of maidens, honey kisses of
   fair ones
And singing ones – and that sufficeth!

HO HOILIGEAN, HO M' AIGHEAN

Eudail thu 's thu dh'an chrodh mhara,
Chra chluasach, bheum chluasach, bheannach;
Chrathadh fual aìr cruach do sheanar,
'S cha tar thu uam⁄s' a Luan no Sha'urn.
    Ho hoiligean, ho m' aighean!
    Ho hoiligean, ho m' aighean!
    Ho hoiligean, ho m' aighean!
    Mo lochruidh chaomh gach taobh an abhuinn.

Eudail thu 's thu chrodh na tire,
Bheir thu marrum, bheir thu mis dhomh;
Bheir thu bainne barr na ciob dhomh,
'S cha b' e glaisle ghlas an t⁄siobain.
    Ho hoiligean, ho m' aighean!

Eudail thu 's thu chrodh an t⁄saoghail,
Bheir thu bainne barr an fhraoich dhomh;
Cha bhainne glas air bhlas a chaorain,
Ach bainne meal 's e air gheal na faoileig.
    Ho hoiligean, ho m' aighean!

Bheir Bride bhinn dhut linn is ograidh,
Bheir Moire mhin dhut li dha d' chomhdach,
Bheir Michael liobha dhut ri dha d' sheoladh,
'S bheir Iosda Criosda dhut sith is solas.
    Ho hoiligean, ho m' aighean!

HO HOILIGEAN, HO MY HEIFERS

My treasure thou, and thou art of the sea kine,
Red eared, notch eared, high horned;
Urine was sprinkled on the rump of thy grandsire,
And thou shalt not win from me on Monday nor Saturday.
　　Ho hoiligean, ho my heifers!
　　Ho hoiligean, ho my heifers!
　　Ho hoiligean, ho my heifers!
　　My kindly kine on each side of the stream.

My treasure thou, and thou art of the land kine,
Thou wilt give me milk produce, thou wilt give me dainty;
Thou wilt give me milk from the top of the club-moss,
And not the grey water of the sand-drift.
　　Ho hoiligean, ho my heifers!

My treasure thou, and thou art of the world's kine,
Thou wilt give me milk from the heather tops;
Not grey milk of the taste of the rowan berries,
But honey milk and white as the sea-gull.
　　Ho hoiligean, ho my heifers!

The melodious Bride will give thee offspring and young,
The lovely Mary will give thee colour to cover thee,
The lustrous Michael will give thee a star to guide thee,
And Christ Jesu will give thee peace and joy.
　　Ho hoiligean, ho my heifers!

With so much unavoidable toil packed into the hours of daylight, there was little time for recreation. At sundown, the evening star glittered in the luminous twilight, the night bird called and the working dogs curled thankfully to rest; the beasts came down from the hill and the folk from the field, and the boats glided silently into safe harbour. In the croft the cook-ing pot, which always included the 'stranger's share', was on the peat fire, and many a stranger paid generously with songs and tales, in exchange for a 'bite'. And the women would knit quietly. As the rune of hospitality says:

'I saw a stranger yestreen; I put food in the eating place, drink in the drinking place, music in the listening place; and, in the sacred name of the Triune, He blessed myself and my house, my cattle and my dear ones. And the lark said in her song, Often, often, often, goes the Christ in the stranger's guise.'

BEANNACHADH SMALAIDH

Smalaidh mis an tula
Mar a smaladh Muire;
Comraig Bhride 's Mhuire,
Air an tula 's air an lar,
    'S air an fhardaich uile.

Co siud air liana mach?
Muire ghrian-gheal 's a Mac,
Bial Dia dh' iarradh, aingheal Dia labhradh;
Ainghle geallaidh faire an teallaidh,
    Gu'n tig latha geal gu beallaidh.

SMOORING BLESSING

I will smoor the hearth
As Mary would smoor;
The encompassment of Bride and of Mary,
On the fire and on the floor,
    And on the household all.

Who is on the lawn without?
Fairest Mary and her Son,
The mouth of God ordained, the angel of God spoke;
Angels of promise watching the hearth,
    Till white day comes to the fire.

CUSTOMS

In the islands the betrothal contract or booking, *leuruch,* was a time of much speculation and anticipation which merited a celebration of its own, quite apart from the wedding or nuptial feast. The young couple having gained prior consent, a straightforward agreement on all sides could be sealed with a dram of whisky for all those present, while the happy couple drank from the same vessel in token of their bond.

Marriage by Declaration, when a couple simply stated that they were man and wife, was perfectly valid until the law was changed in 1939. However, the islanders preferred the formal 'asking' for the girl followed by the betrothal feast. It was an open secret who had decided on whom; the girl's father had to be asked by the suitor who was supported by his best friend who spoke on his behalf. In most cases the girl showed willing by hovering in the background and accepting her future partner after the formal proposal. Depending on the circumstances a bride price could be demanded – this has been a custom for centuries in many lands – and hard bargaining took place between the menfolk concerned.

Long ago it was customary to ask the MacNeill to supply a suitable partner for any of his people who were either bereaved or single, who wished his help with the selection. It was not unusual for a lonely shy widower to solicit the help of a friend to deputise for him with a proposal of marriage, or for fathers with 'stay-at-home' sons to suggest that it was time to 'bring home a wife to help'.

After the formal betrothal the wedding was fixed when the 'moon was waxing and the tide flowing' – to give luck to the couple. They selected two trusty kinsmen, a girl and a man, to assist with the preparations, the first of which was the delivery to each house of the personal invitation. The bride and bridegroom invited the relatives and close friends, while their two helpers called on anyone else, being careful that no one was forgotten, as this was considered a grave insult.

One young man gave such a liberal betrothal party, the whisky flowing like water, that at the height of the festivities a brawl started which lasted till daybreak with many a broken head and tooth. He was so frightened by the formidable reprisals suggested by some of his guests that he ran away and joined a ship, returning twenty years later to marry the bride.

Betrothals were short, with perhaps two or three weeks before the marriage ceremony, and if the groom was a fisherman he had on no account to go to sea meanwhile. The story goes that one man about to be married ignored this superstition and continued fishing from one port to another. All went well until he came in sight of his future mother-in-law's house, when a large bee came whirring past the boat; immediately, a strong squall of wind threw the boat on its beam ends, whereupon they returned to port with all speed. The mother-in-law disapproved of the marriage and was an uncanny person as well so he was afraid she might sink the boat. He again attempted to go to sea the day before the wedding, with his friends doing their utmost to prevent him. As soon as the boat started it was driven by waves onto a sandbank – where it had to remain, as he was thrown overboard and had to make the best of his way home!

The approach of the wedding or nuptial celebration was a time of great activity and gaiety with most friends contributing something towards the feast. This involved serving so many guests that they had to be fed in relays. If there was a house large enough

it was used, otherwise tables were placed in a barn or on the grass outside. The bridegroom provided whisky which flowed copiously, while six or seven sheep could be killed and roasted along with many fowls and fish. There were potatoes and bannocks, with a piece of butter and cheese for each guest. Toasts were drunk from overflowing beakers and there was great conviviality, all present being filled with happiness and elated with hope in new beginnings. Highland hospitality to neighbours and kinsmen alike has no bounds.

In the nineteenth century repeated volleys of musketry summoned the guests to the ceremony and were fired over the couple when they emerged after the 'Hymenal' knot was tied. The revelry lasted all through the day and most of the night with reels and dancing until the rafters began to revolve. The bride and groom were escorted, by all the kinsmen and guests who could still stand, to a 'shake down' or rough mattress on the floor of a barn, as it was the custom to begin married life in a state of humility. In Barra both mothers sprinkled holy water on the marriage bed and blessed it.

Youthful enthusiasm and gaiety lighten the work load when life is 'real and very earnest', so the Festival of Saint Barr on 25th September was eagerly anticipated by the community. This appears to have changed to The Festival of Saint Michael in the seventeenth century. After Mass in the early morning each man went, on horseback with his wife or favourite girl riding behind him, in procession three times 'sunwise' round the sacred church of Kilbar. This ceremony was followed by the eating of cakebread or bannocks and probably some fish, while the younger women provided wild field carrots for the men. The bannocks were made using the first grain of the year, with the introduction of a little of each cereal grown on the croft. Every member of the household including visitors was expected to eat a piece. These bannocks are still baked using ordinary flour and treacle with the additional flavouring of caraway seed and currants. The rest of the day was spent on games, horse racing, shinty matches and dancing. The young men rode races with skill and great hilarity as neither saddle nor bridle were allowed. If they did not own a horse it was permitted on that day to borrow one anywhere, even without asking permission.

Although perpetuated until the middle of the nineteenth century, this happy custom died out, probably at the time of the crop famine and the evictions, when misery was widespread. The mysterious disappearance of the much venerated statue of Saint Barr makes today's islanders smile, as rumour has it that the statue which was used to dress the church was the figurehead of a wrecked ship.

Family life with its births, marriages and deaths was lightened with a tune and a song to give a lift and rhythm to every chore from milking and churning to spinning and weaving. The *ceilidh* (pronounced cay-lee) is built into the island culture and has been a part of life for centuries. The *ceilidh* can be held anywhere and for special occasions may be staged in the island school with the audience sitting in neat rows, but the informality of a private house or the local bar is more appropriate to the spontaneous nature of this event. However, the recently established Barra Festival *Feis Bharraidh* has an appeal of its own, set as it is in the open, with beautiful island scenery as a background.

One of the first Barramen to take an academic interest in the music of the pipes was Calum Johnston who, with two other Barramen, held a prominent place among Scottish pipers in Edinburgh. Many of

the performers at the present-day Festival are from Barra, although it attracts a wide circle of talents from the mainland.

The Islanders excel at reminiscing and having a good gossip round the warm fire. Tobacco has always been greatly prized on the islands and the old black houses reeked of it. Probably brought by ships, it was bartered for cloth, feathers or fish. How it was originally handled when it first appeared is anybody's guess but as time passed, the tobacco was possibly treated with alcohol and treacle and bound tightly with tarry twine – navy style. It was a slow-burning, cool and powerfully aromatic smoke which eventually became known as Black Twist and Bogey Roll. Cut with a knife into 'quids' it was greatly relished and either chewed or smoked in a pipe. At one time it was kept in long thin rolls (twist) and purchased by the inch before weighing.

Uisge-beatha, (water of life) or whisky, was medicinal as well as liberating from illness and the daily toil. A relatively new drink, the people were officially allowed to distil it for themselves after 1609. Long ago there were no doctors and life was hard. With many miles of rough country separating the clachans, the *deoch an dorus* was the drink of the door, given

to the guest as he left the dwelling. If the weary islander, wrapped in his plaid, fell asleep in the heather, the protective effect of *uisge-beatha* was thought to drive away evil humours. In these wrapped plaids Barramen braved the severest storms, sleeping rough, even in the snow. They had the greatest contempt for pillows or blankets, so that when choice or necessity induced them to travel they threw aside the bed covers of their hosts, wrapped themselves in their plaids and then slept – afraid lest the barbarian luxuries should contaminate their native hardiness.

The long drawn-out winters with seemingly endless darkness, gales and constant rain helped to create a closely integrated social community. There was a strong element of fear in people's lives and it was thought wiser to add to any statement, 'If all is well' or 'God willing'.

As might be expected, the Barramen are expert seamen and considered the best boatmen in the Western Isles. Long ago when frail boats of wood braved the Atlantic, the men were said to be made of steel and the poems of Ossian glorified their qualities. Over the past eighty years since the failure of the herring industry, the menfolk have had to sail the seas of the world in order to earn a living, returning home only once a year, so naturally the affairs of the family and the island have had to be managed by womenfolk. The women have been activists especially since their hard life as 'crewmen' in the herring-gutting days. Before Sylvia Pankhurst chained herself to the palace railings, Barra women were already striking for an extra penny a barrel – divided between three crew members!

In the absence of the father of the family, the priest often was called in to deliberate, *in loco parentis*, on family decisions, so his importance in the community remained paramount.

Gum bi iad nas gile na eala nam fonn,
Gum bi iad nas gile na faoileag nan tonn,
Gum bi iad nas gile na sneachda nam beann,
Agus nas gile na gràdh geal nan sonn;

Till they are whiter than the swan of the songs,
Till they are whiter than the seagull of the waves,
Till they are whiter than the snow of the peaks,
And whiter than the white love of the heroes.

BEANNACHADH FUIRIRIDH

A lasair leith, chaol, chrom,
Tighinn a toll mhullach nam fod,
A lasair leumrach, leathann, theith,
Na teid le do chleid da m' choir.

Gabhail reidh, sheimh, shuairce,
Tighinn mu 'n cuart mo thetheann,
Teine cubhr, caon, cuana,
Nach dean smur, no smuar, no reubann.

Teasaich, cruadhaich mo shiol miamh,
Chon biadh dha mo leanu‿beag,
An ainm Chriosda, Righ nan sian,
Thug duinn iodh, is iadh, is beannachd leis,
 An ainm Chriosda, Righ nan sian,
  Thug duinn iodh, is iadh, is beannachd leis.

THE BLESSING OF THE PARCHING

Thou flame grey, slender, curved,
Coming from the top pore of the peat,
Thou flame of leaps, breadth, heat,
Come not nigh me with thy quips.

A burning steady, gentle, generous,
Coming round about my quicken roots,
A fire fragrant, fair, and peaceful,
Nor causes dust, nor grief, nor havoc.

Heat, parch my fat seed,
For food for my little child,
In name of Christ, King of the elements,
Who gave us corn and bread and blessing withal,
 In name of Christ, King of the elements,
  Who gave us corn and bread and blessing withal.

SUPERSTITIONS

At the heart of all superstition is the belief in a religious origin. The people loved and admired deities who brought them good luck and plenty, and hated and feared those whom they thought caused disaster and suffering.

The Druids persuaded the people to believe that some families had been enchanted and changed into beasts and as the proper charms had not been used, the spell had never been broken; that swans, seals and mermaids had been human before being enchanted.

There were also witches, who could communicate with evil spirits from whom they received the power to change themselves into any shape they pleased; they often changed into beasts when there was some evil design in view and it was very dangerous to meet them. It was thought they could take away the produce of a dairy and sometimes of the whole farm.

Druid legends and superstitions are very well known and it is possible that tales invented by them were told as sermons; that for payment they could produce charms to prevent evil and disease and to break the spell of fairies and witches who could spirit them away, or harm or annoy them. They pretended to be friends of the people, but the tales invented to frighten and intimidate were the ones which they carefully preserved.

Druids called their God *beil* or *beul* and the miracles which they claimed were called beil-fingering – their magic, druidism. Superstitions of Druidical origin, built around the elemental facts of existence – fire, water, life and death, are still with us today and are almost as mysterious as they were to early mankind. Fire is a sacred Druid mystery and we still say ... 'he is between two fires' when someone is in a dilemma, not realising we refer to the fires of Baal or Belus. There is a Gaelic saying 'Who steals the fire steals the blessing', while Hallowe'en is a Druid 'fire feast'.

At the first sign of winter the people gathered to make a huge blaze or bonfire to defeat witches and evil spirits or at least deprive them of the power to plunder the produce of the farm. All fires were extinguished and the hearths allowed to grow cold before a *teine figin* or 'Fire of Need' was lit, which had many uses. The Druids said that it was not safe to kindle fire unless it was bought from a *beil*'s Druid which, of course, was extortion. This 'special' fire was named *beil-teine* (Beil's fire) or Holy Fire. It was started by the ancient method of rubbing wood to produce a flame which rekindled the peat on the cold hearth.

As recently as 1800, fishermen huddled together the night before the fishing season started, taking part in this ceremony, from which they would carry away a small piece of kindling to their own homes. The kindling was also used to light a large fire outside through the smoke of which any cattle exposed to the plague or infection were driven, as a precaution to ensure their good health. Branches of the rowan tree tied with red thread in the form of a cross, were considered a potent charm against evil spirits, particularly when placed in the 'midden' or inserted into the door lintels of dwellings.

The young people had their own fun at Beltane, a festival in honour of the return of the sun with its warmth. While their elders and betters were consumed with anxiety for the safety of their cattle, crops, and homes and families, the children lit a huge fire on the moorland and baked a large bannock which was cut into pieces to equal the number present. One piece was blackened with ashes and put with the rest into a bag. Each child, blindfolded in turn, chose a piece and whoever drew the black bit was the person doomed to be sacrificed to Baal. In order to avoid the execution of his or her 'doom', the victim was compelled to leap six times over the flames. Another popular game was to cut the sign of life (or cross) on one side of each piece of bannock and a cypher (of death) on the other. Then the bannocks were arranged in a line and allowed to run down a hill and this caper was repeated three times. If the cross landed uppermost more often than the cypher, the child concerned would live for another year, but if it was the cypher – the victim was doomed to die. Beltane bannocks were originally cakes baked as an offering to propitiate the Goddess of Heaven, but Saint Columba saw the advantage of adding the

Christian Cross and so concealed their pagan origin; they became Easter symbols called Hot Cross Buns.

At this time the wives sang the Gaelic Beltane Blessing to the 'fire of peace':

Bless O threefold true and beautiful – Myself, my
    spouse and my children,
My tender children and the beloved mother at their
    head,
On the fragrant plain, on the gay mountain sheiling.
Everything in my dwelling or in my possession, all
    Kine and crops, all flocks and corn,
From Hallow Eve to Beltane Eve, With goodly
    progress and gentle blessing
From sea to sea, and every river mouth
From wave to wave, and base of waterfall.

ACHLASAN CHALUIM-CHILLE

Achlasain Chaluim-chille,
Gun sireadh, gun iarraidh,
Achlasain Chaluim-chille,
Fo m' righe gu siorruidh!

Air Shealbh dhaona,
Air shealbh mhaona,
Air shealbh mhianna,
Air shealbh chaora,
Air shealbh mhaosa,
Air shealbh iana,
Air shealbh raona,
Air shealbh mhaora,
Air shealbh iasga,
Air shealbh bhliochd is bhuar,
Air shealbh shliochd is shluagh,
Air shealbh bhlar is bhuadh,
Air tir, air lir, air cuan,
Trid an Tri ta shuas,
Trid an Tri ta nuas,
Trid an Tri ta buan,
Achlasain Chaluim-chille,
Ta mis a nis da d' bhuain,
    Ta mis a nis da d' bhuain.

ST COLUMBA'S PLANT

Plantlet of Columba,
Without seeking, without searching,
Plantlet of Columba,
Under my arm for ever!

For luck of men,
For luck of means,
For luck of wish (?),
For luck of sheep,
For luck of goats,
For luck of birds,
For luck of fields,
For luck of shell-fish,
For luck of fish,
For luck of produce and kine,
For luck of progeny and people,
For luck of battle and victory,
On land, on sea, on ocean,
Through the Three on high,
Through the Three a-nigh,
Through the Three eternal,
Plantlet of Columba,
I cull thee now,
    I cull thee now.

Beira, the winter queen, could and did bring snow and ice and raise mighty storms, but she had no power to prevent the trees budding or the grass growing in the spring. She was the goddess of mountains, lochs and rivers as well as of the weather until she was overthrown by Bride, the Goddess of Spring. On 'Brides Day', the first day of the Gaelic Spring, offerings were made to the earth and sea. Milk was poured on the ground and the fisher folk made porridge and threw it into the sea. The gods and goddesses of ancient times were rarely carved as statues, and would have been completely forgotten centuries ago but for the old bards with their songs, poems and tales, while the changing seasons were thought to be caused by unnamed powers.

Proceeding clockwise, 'the way of the sun', is considered lucky and is part of the ancient worship of Baal, while the opposite direction, 'widdershins', is thought to be unlucky. How many card players realise that the dealer is following this ritual? We stir our cooking pots 'deiseil' or sunwise and the wine at the dinner table is always circulated likewise 'the way of the sun'. And so we are still under the influence of the Druids, performing acts from long forgotten ancient days.

There are holy, healing and wishing wells all over Scotland although there is little evidence, apart from the two wells within Kishmul Castle, that places more than one of them in Barra. 'The Well of Virtues', *Tobbar Nam Buadh*, was supposed to have medicinal value and also to cure the effects of witchcraft. There are of course a few mineral springs scattered about the Barra Isles. Nearly all our old wells are of Druidical origin and were considered to be inhabited by a deity. Many appear to be Christian as Saint Columba was adept at grafting the new faith onto the old. Amongst many things the Druids

invoked were sacred trees, tools and wells. Water was also sacred, in all its forms – snow, dew, rain, rivers, springs and wells.

Holy wells were considered especially potent at Hallowe'en and May time, while the Druids believed that 'dew' was the most sacred of all water forms, and it was carefully collected in hollowed-out stones. To wash in the precious May Day dew ensured good luck, sanity and beauty of face for a year. The elements of fire and water follow the Celt from birth to death and a bargain made over water is indissoluble, hence the farmer or trader spits on the hand before striking a deal.

The use of the healing wells was thought to be most effective during the summer period until September, as the cures prescribed would not only be most uncomfortable, but possibly fatal if carried out in winter. There is a story of two friends, both delicate in health. One of them died and the other was desparately unhappy. One day he thought he heard his friend's voice telling him to go to a certain rock not far away and that he would meet him there, but alas, no one appeared. There was a bee flying nearby and he thought it said to him, 'Dig, Willie and drink'. So he did and when the first piece of turf was torn up a spring of pure water gushed out. He at once drank of it and was cured of his consumption.

Sometimes pebbles are supposed to give healing powers to lochs: 'To be sure of a cure it is necessary for the patients to come to the edge of the loch about midnight on the first Monday of May or August, wait for the first streak of dawn and then strip themselves in silence. As they enter the loch they throw in a coin and allow the water to close over their heads three times, earnestly wishing to be cured the while. Next, they dress in silence and if possible walk round

the loch sunwise. They then depart, taking good care to be out of sight of the loch before sunrise.'

The cold bath was so much esteemed by the Highlanders in ancient times that, as soon as an infant was born, he was plunged into a running stream and then carefully wrapped in a warm blanket. Immediately thereafter, the infant was forced to swallow a large quantity of fresh butter. It was rolled into a ball and pressed down the throat to the near suffocation of the child. An idea prevalent when a child was baptised was that it should not be bathed that night, for fear of washing off the baptismal water before it had slept under it.

Many of the old customs are now obsolete having been replaced by today's scientific knowledge. Nevertheless the old ideas were often founded on facts that were not fully understood at the time.

The rhythmical cycle of the seasons was closely followed, as the islanders were influenced to a greater or lesser degree by the phases of the moon, which indicated the changing seasons; the crop-rotation, when the herds should go out to pasture, to the shieling, or their return in the autumn, the fishing and the movement of the herring, the tides and the rowing. The best time to cut the peat, sow the crops, make dykes and cut rushes for thatching were all ordained by the seasons. Likewise it was considered very unlucky to cut hair, even a lock from a child, when the moon was waxing. As in Ecclesiastes, everything had its own time. Nevertheless, the invisible 'little people' could be about. They were very politely referred to as Men of Peace, *Daoine Sith*, because they might just carry off a new-born baby and replace it with a changeling, or shoot flint barbs at the cattle. It was better not to antagonise them, and even today, one can't be too careful.

In some districts the belief lingered that there were men and women who had the power to do harm by merely looking at those they disliked. It is not to be wondered at that the teaching of Christianity, 'Thou shalt not covet', has redirected this superstition, so that its cure is to invoke the Deity and the Holy Trinity. The Gaelic proverb, 'The eye of the envious will split the stone', is perfectly portrayed by this tale.

A long time ago a man was carrying a quern or hand corn-mill on his back in a poke (small bag) and was met by a servant of Saint Columba. Thinking the quern was a cheese, he coveted it and when the man came to take out the stone he found it broken in two.

Such people were regarded as dangerous. When any had been 'struck by the evil eye' they became sick, drowsy and faded away until they were skeletons. Cows 'struck' ceased to give milk; other cattle had accidents which destroyed them; if fishermen were 'overlooked', they caught very little while others had plenty and so the household was threatened with ruin. Fortunately there was always some person with the power to frustrate this dire problem, known as the *eolas* person. *Eolas* is also Gaelic for charm, or an incantation which was spoken over the remedy for the good of the sufferer.

Consultations with a physician or veterinary surgeon were extremely rare in isolated places and consequently the person who had *eolas* was also a faith healer using herbs and potions but mostly invoking the blessing of God. Children were at special risk from the curse of 'the eye' which was associated with witchcraft.

A newly born baby had a knife placed in its cradle to ward off evil and the day of birth was important, giving a clue to the child's future.

Sunday's child is full of grace, Monday's child is
  full of face,
Tuesday's child is solemn and sad, Wednesday's
  child is merry and glad.
Thursday's child is inclined to thieving, Friday's
  child is free in giving.
'Saturday's child works hard for its living.'

It was believed that a child born after midnight might
grow to be 'uncanny' with partial 'second sight' or
extra sensory perception, an idea which in later life
exposed some unfortunates to the accusation of wiz-
ardry or witchcraft. An accepted safeguard was to
ask a blessing upon oneself or upon the occupants
of a house and the livestock, particularly the cow and
the milk, which is still done to this day.

The smoke from a fire of juniper wood was
another cure, and cattle were protected by a small
piece of rowan tree tied to the tail with a black cloth
bound by blue yarn; sometimes it was tied round
a cow's horns or neck. Burning a small piece of cloth
and throwing it after a departing person would get
rid of 'the eye'. Another prevention was to wear a
piece of clothing inside-out, or wave a small burning

stick or peat over and around clothing as a purification. A touch of tar in the ears, noses and horns of cattle prevented injuries on May Eve (which makes good sense today as flies do lay their eggs on the noses of cattle). A piece cut out of the ear of a dead beast would prevent 'the eye' affecting the rest of the cattle; what was good for cows was also good for horses. Urine too was a deterrant.

Many different devices were used as charms against evil, the most common being a red thread about five inches long which was procured from the *eolas* person. The giver said 'some good words over it' and the thread was tied on to the cattle, horses' tails and even round the necks of children where it would remain for many days until the cure was effected. The words of the incantations as translated by Dr. Maclagan are:

'Let the evil that afflicted him be driven by the winds afar: And let him arise in strength and hope and joy, to magnify the goodness of the most high. With water of silver, from swiftly running stream I sprinkle thee. Arise and be well.'

TATAN BEOTHAICH

Ioba 'ga chur ad chluais dheis
   Gu do leas is chan ann gu t'aimhleas;
Gaol na fearainn tha fo d' chois,
   Is fuath na fuinn bho'n d'fhalbh thu.

Tha fois aig mo ghaol a nochd
   Am fochara nam farrabheann;
Do cheangal teann am làimh nochd,
   Tha glas iarainn ort, a Tharragheal.

Water had to be taken to a sufferer in the name of the Trinity from a ford or crossing where 'the living and dead pass'. Silver, gold or copper were then added, usually coins, but a ring, brooch or earring would do. The person or beast was made to drink a mouthful or two of the water and the rest was sprinkled all over the body.

When a person was 'out of sorts' as they say, he was considered a suitable subject for the silver water cure. A female well advanced in life was usually the operator and she produced from her store a silver coin, the larger the better, or a silver brooch with interlacements. Getting a wooden or earthenware bowl, she would fill the vessel from the nearest running stream to the depth of the second joint of her middle finger when dipped straight down into the water. Into this she would put the coin or brooch then go 'in a straight course' to the one upon whom the charm was to be wrought. Great care had to be taken not to spill a drop and the straighter the course the greater the success. The 'patient' was then made to lie on his back, chest and neck bare, while the woman stood over him with the bowl of silver water in her left hand. Dipping the forefinger of her right hand in

ATTRACTING AN ANIMAL

The spell is placed in thy right ear
   For thy good and not for thy harm;
Love of the land that is under thy foot,
   And dislike of the land thou hast left.

My love has rest this night
   Hard by the mountain ridges;
Thy fast binding in my bare hand,
   An iron lock is upon thee, 'Breast-white.'

the water, she made the sign of the cross upon his forehead and in a low voice repeated an incantation. During this, with her right hand she sprinkled water as rapidly as possible, seven times over the 'patient'. There would only be enough left to cover the coins, which the 'patient' would drink to the last drop, tilting the bowl until the coins touched his lips and he was confident that he had been cured.

On the islands a young calf was often more highly prized than a child and given unstinting care and food for its survival. There are many stories about the animals, as one collector recalled.

'My mother, remembering my grandfather's cow, put spring water in a luggie pouch with a silver and a copper coin and a darning needle. She forced some of the water down the calf's throat and sprinkled the rest over it. The calf recovered and the farmer's wife

was so delighted. "Well, well, I never saw the like before, you can do anything!" she said.' The needle with its eye is an obvious charm.

It is hard to believe that an Act of Scottish Parliament in 1563 made witchcraft a capital offence. So-called witches received the most hideous punishment, in thousands of cases quite undeservedly. A woman only needed to be a little eccentric (and perhaps a nature-lover collecting herbs) – poor and not very clean, for her to be stoned and declared a witch. Alleged witches were 'cut above the breath', which was done with a knife or sharp instrument to prevent them doing harm; there was an example of this in 1750 when a woman and her daughter were dragged out of bed, thrown to the ground and held down by men, while others 'scored and cut their foreheads with an iron tool, shouting and calling them witches.'

A simple remedy for a bewitched cow was to put a silver coin or ring into a basin of water and then sprinkle it over the animal. If she shook herself it was thought the treatment had been successful but if not, a gold coin was substituted and the operation repeated. If the cow still did not shake herself, then a pail of water was brought from the stream and 'seven blades' dipped into it, and if she was quiescent after this the case was regarded as hopeless. The water of 'seven blades' was made by putting seven sharp-pointed instruments into the water. Pins, pocket knives, etc. did quite well. Witches were reputed to cross rivers and lochs in egg shells and this is the reason why after eating an egg the spoon is usually pushed through the shell, thus preventing its use. If a woman was a masculine type with enough hair on her face to make a schoolboy envious, and especially if she lived alone, preferably in a deserted place, or was deaf, dumb, cunning or malevolent, she was firmly established as a witch.

In the Highlands and Islands many people are under the power of a certain kind of vision called 'The second sight'; they can predict unexpected and wonderful events by this power which is beyond their control and in many cases not a welcome 'gift'. Dr. Johnson has written a good definition in his 'Journey to the Western Isles of Scotland'. 'The second sight is an impression made either by the mind on the eye, or by the eye on the mind, by which things distant and future are received and seen as if they were present.'

Seers are know to exist all over the world, particularly in remote underpopulated areas where quiet lives are favourable to the formation of strange beliefs, but the second sight must not be confused with the 'Evil Eye' which is known to be a superstition. The phenomenon of the 'second sight' is taken seriously as predictions foretelling adversity or prosperity have proved to be correct, times without number. Islanders may shrug their shoulders and laugh at such things but superstitions connected with the sea are still observed and they will not deliberately flout customs which have been handed down from generation to generation.

In the Hebrides, when the boats left to fish on the east coast, a cat – so the story goes – was put in a bag and kept there without food or water until word was received of their safe arrival; and fishermen's wives had to be careful when baking oatcakes not to blow away any oatmeal – if they wish to avoid a hurricane blowing their husbands off the sea! Also it was thought that to throw into the fire any part of a fish, even the bones, would cause the fish to be scarce for the fishing.

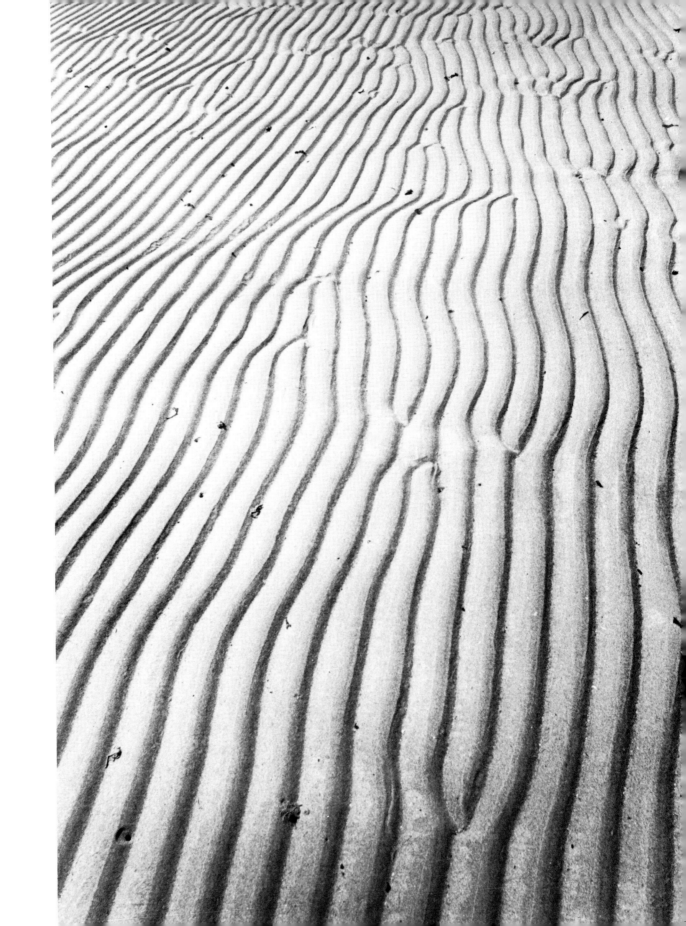

'Chualas nuall an cuan Canach,
Bo a Tiriodh, bo a Barraidh,
Bo a Ile, 's bo a Arainn,
'S a Cinntire uain a bharraich.

Caillear, caillear, caillear Cuachag,
Caillear Gumag, caillear Guamag.
Caillear Guileag, caillear Guaillionn,
'S caillear Cruinneag dhonn na buaile.

Theid mi, theid mi, theid mi Mhuile,
Theid mi dh' Eire nam fear fuileach,
Theid mi Mhannain bheag nan culaidh,
'S theid mi ceum dh'an Fhraing 's cha rbunnart.

Caillear, caillear, caillear Gorag,
Caillear Dubhag, caillear Dothag,
Caillear Muileag, caillear Moileag,
'S caillear Muirneag dhonn an orf built.'

A low is heard in the sea of Canna,
A cow from Tiree, a cow from Barra,
A cow from Islay, a cow from Arran,
And from green Kintyre of birches.

Lost, lost, lost will be 'Cuachag,'
Lost will be 'Gumag,' lost will be 'Guamag,'
Lost will be 'Guileag,' lost will be 'Guaillionn,'
And brown 'Cruinneag' of the cattlefold.

I will go, I will go, I will go to Mull,
I will go to Eirin of the bloody men,
I will go to little Man of the wherries,
And I will go to France and no mishap.

Lost, lost, lost will be 'Gorag,'
Lost will be 'Dubhag,' lost will be 'Dothag,'
Lost will be 'Muileag,' lost will be 'Moileag,'
And brown 'Muirneag' of the golden hair.

The Gaelic proverb 'There is no disease without a remedy, and no turning back from death' is balanced by the proverb 'Man by nature is healthy'. Having taken all reasonable precautions to prevent undesirable events, the people accepted the inevitable with a fatalistic 'It had to be'. Nine times out of ten the patient was not sure what was wrong with him and the 'doctor' could not promise a cure although professing to know the functions of every part of the human body, and also the temperament of the patient; one of the first things she took care to notice (for women formed the bulk of the profession) were peculiar birth marks or moles.

The 'doctor' engaged in chatter about weather, fishing or crops before cautiously approaching the object of the visit. The disease suspected was named and a woollen thread was wound three times round a horn spoon and the ends placed together. This was passed thrice round the hook (which suspended the pots over the fire). If the thread fell off, the patient did not have that particular disease and this process was repeated and 'named' until the thread stayed on, after which it was 'apply the usual remedies!' Hanging coloured rags on neighbouring trees was not absolutely necessary, although this was considered 'leaving the trouble behind', while to remove a rag was to assume responsibility oneself for the trouble of the person who had hung it there.

Epilepsy was thought the work of evil spirits which had to be exorcised if possible. One remedy was to reverently take a black cock, and kill and bury it carefully where the first attack had taken place, with incantations being repeated during the ceremony. With another, the parings of toe and finger nails were wrapped up in a cloth with a new sixpence and the words of the Trinity and placed under the wing of a black cock, which was carried backwards to the place of the first fit, and buried alive by the oldest God-fearing man in the district, who watched all night by an unquenchable fire kindled above the cock. Another gruesome remedy was to drink water out of the skull of a suicide. Common diseases such as measles, scarlet fever and whooping cough became extremely virulent when introduced to isolated communities and the people of Barra dreaded and feared 'fever'. Any house with fever would literally be avoided as if it were the plague. Returning sailors brought malaria, known as the 'shivering fever', *Fiobhras-criothanach*, and there are stories of epidemics which were probably typhoid or typhus, but as the inhabitants were well spaced out these were localized and the islands were never devastated. No one would venture into infected houses except the priest and, nearer our own time, the doctor.

There was one time when the MacNeill became concerned about the people of Mingulay as there had been no word from the island over a long period, so he sent a boat to investigate. On its arrival, a man called Macphee was landed and he made the awful discovery that the dwellings contained nothing but corpses, as everyone had died of the plague (probably typhus). Horror-struck, he ran back to the boat but the crew, fearing contamination, refused to take him aboard and sailed away leaving him marooned alone with the dead.

Miraculously he survived, and a year later when MacNeill again sent a boat, Macphee was rescued, resettled and compensated with a grant of land. He related the anguish of his ordeal and how day after day he had climbed an eight hundred and ninety one-foot hill to watch for a relief ship to rescue him. Ever since then the incline has been known as Macphee's Hill.

Tuberculosis or as it was known on the islands, consumption, the 'wasting disease' took a heavy toll and in the olden days snails were finely chopped and hung before the fire in a flannel bag to drip on marrow, which was swallowed in tablespoon doses. Jelly was made from the scrapings of deer's horns which were dissolved and drunk, while nettle and heather tops were also brewed.

Whooping cough was treated by the sufferer wearing a hairy caterpillar in a small bag round the neck, or asking the advice of a person riding a white or piebald pony, and great faith was placed in drinking from the horn broken off any animal.

Jaundice was treated by water taken from the top of the ninth wave in which nine stones were boiled. The patient's shirt was then dipped in the water and put on wet. Also very effective was water taken from nine streams in which grew nine cresses.

Toothache was cured by rising early, carrying an earthworm in the mouth, and walking four miles!

Sore eyes were cured by rubbing with a gold ring or being brushed with a black hair, but the best effect was from bathing with a concoction of the plant eye-bright (euphorbia). A 'black eye' was cured by a slice of raw potato and gold earrings worn by both sexes prevented sore eyes.

The proper treatment for smallpox was eating a fried mouse accompanied by whisky or black beer and, not without justification, whisky was looked upon as the universal solvent of misfortune, much as it is today. Some comfort, if not a cure, could be had from most faith healers, the body having incredible powers of recovery and resistance. There was good sense in the Gaelic proverb, 'Health is an inheritance to be bequeathed to one's children'.

CEILIDHS & FOLKLORE

On winter nights it was the custom in small villages or clachans for friends to collect in a house and hold what they called a *ceilidh*. The Goodman of the house, *Fear an Tigh*, usually opened the proceedings with a 'Tale of a Great Giant', or some well-known favourite, after which everyone present was expected to contribute. Personal anecdotes and the quoting of sayings were greatly relished, while the asking of riddles and puzzles caused much merriment. There was a relaxed friendly gaiety and conviviality with plenty of witty remarks bandied about. The songs were often wild and beautiful telling of love or war, composed on the spot like a calypso, with a particular rhyme, and often pibroch-style mouth music.

In the olden days there was a rush to secure a good place as the *ceilidh* was always 'round the fire'. In the centre of the room dogs, maybe a cat and possibly a few hens jostled for positions near the warmth. As recorded in the nineteenth century by J. F. Campbell; 'The rest of the dwelling faded away through the blue mist of the peat smoke, through shades of deepening brown, to the black darkness of the smoked roof and the 'peat corner'. There we sat and smoked and talked for hours till the tide ebbed; and then I crossed the ford by wading up to the waist and dried my clothes in the wind of the island.'

The tailor and shoemaker travelled from house to house passing on information and gossip, but mostly telling stories, and accordingly one could judge their ability by the size of the audience. The islanders listened attentively to the tales of freebooters who came and plundered, taking cattle, and to how their ancestors would gather to protect their property; the battles, the dress they wore, the kind of weapons used and the different hardships they had to endure. The most popular tales described very rapid changes of place and heroic romances which excited strong emotions, with tears giving way to the loud laughter of relief. One tailor engaged in making many garments had a different tale for every night of his stay. Told sitting round the peat fire the tales were handed down by word of mouth from father to son. Few could read or write as there was very little formal education and therefore the stories were learnt with great accuracy. They are an insight into primitive thought, folklore and philosophy, describing the living conditions, habits and history of the people. The story-teller was a spinner of dreams, embracing everything beyond the daily toil.

Islanders and Highlanders delight in mystery and the unknown. To them the home of the gods was not situated in unattainable isolation but was of easy access in a mythical manner. If a handsome warrior drew the attention of a goddess he was simply spirited off in a magical way into the centre of a rock or a hill. Access to the immortals was effected by passing through a smoke screen or fog, and time was condensed into flashes. What excitement must have followed the news that a tailor or shoemaker was coming.

The Gaelic tales often resemble the tales from Hans Anderson, or sometimes, 'The Arabian Nights', and many appear to be a mixture from several countries — but the entire setting and decoration are West Highland, as if the tales had grown there. The 'book' stories were brought to the islands, absorbed and transformed into a likeness of the people and their West Highland setting, and stripped of nearly all that was foreign. Each kind of storytelling had its specialist reciter. The peasant 'historian' tells of clan battles, while another knows the descent of most of the families in Scotland and all about his neighbour's origin. Some narrators tell of romances and giants, others are moralists, and a few are anti⁄quarians. Each has his own subject but the best know tales of all kinds. One story grows out of another and with audience participation a tale rambles on.

It was not unusual for a guest at the *ceilidh*, having partaken freely of his host's generous hospitality, to drowse off and awaken the following morning to find that a tale had continued uninterrupted throughout the night and was still unfinished.

Some of the Ossianic romances are presumed to be of great antiquity, for even a tale heard in 1780 contained unknown Gaelic words which were thought at the time to be foreign and were only under⁄

stood by their context within the tale. The most popular lore in the West, which is also known all over the Islands, concerns the tradition of the old history of the Finne: a specially bred 'master race' from Ireland. Elsewhere this lore is called the *Poems of Ossian* and many of these are of great length, sometimes 200 lines, memorised by the recitors and spoken in a rapid chant. There has been much controversy about the old lore, and its traditions and translations, and it is very probable that Ossian did not compose all the poems that are attributed to him. But he was a Gael and most Island folk are content to believe that Ossian was the last of the Finne.

It is easy to see how the Celts' fear of the supernatural excited the imagination. Spine-chilling tales abound of wraithes, apparitions, fairies, witches and spunkies, with kelpies being the worst devils in Gaelic folklore. Fairy music was a dreaded thing as it bewitched the hearer, who disappeared in search of it 'for a year and a day', sometimes never to return.

Thousands of years ago horses were strange, rare and probably sacred amongst the Celts and other races. They appear to have been greatly prized, worshipped and feared; they also had magical properties attributed to them, by which they could assume the form of men or women, and these are frequently mentioned in Gaelic tales. Most dreaded in all Celtic folklore is the *each uisge*, a kelpie or water horse which appears as a destroying water-god devouring its victims after first luring them to their doom. The *each uisge* in the guise of a beautiful bay or grey horse, will graze at a loch-side or river and when he is touched or mounted, rush into the deepest water and devour his rider. People's hands stick to him; if he is harnessed to a plough he drags the team into the loch where he tears the horses to pieces; his back lengthens to carry a number of people. He appears as

an old woman who is bedded with some lovely young girls in a mountain sheiling, and he sucks the blood of them all except one, who escapes by jumping over a burn which he dare not cross. He is killed, and nothing remains except a pool of water.

There is a story of children playing beside a loch when a lovely horse appeared. One boy jumped up on its back and called to the others to join him for a ride. They all clambered up except one who put his finger on the kelpie's head as if to lead it; to his horror he found it was stuck to the horse and he could not take it away; but instantly he remembered what he had heard about the dangerous water horse at a *ceilidh*. He whipped out his knife and hacked off his finger, and so escaped as the kelpie, with all his playmates, rushed into the loch and disappeared.

Another tale is of a kelpie who, in the form of a handsome young man, made love to a farmer's daughter living near to its loch. The girl was deeply attracted and encouraged his advances until one day she accidently spilled some boiling water on his feet. Instead of crying out, he terrified her by whinnying like a horse and kicking out at her. That night she confided the incident to her brothers, who lay in wait for the young man when he came to visit her and quickly dispatched him with their dirks; he screamed and kicked so furiously that he broke one of the brother's legs, but after he died it was not a man but a horse that lay on the ground. They carried the remains into a shed but the following day, when they went to bury it, only a pool of slime remained.

In the earliest accounts of the Western Isles the hound or dog is spoken of in Gaelic poetry. One particular breed was the wire-haired stag-hound, greatly prized by a race of hunters.

An interesting story is told of a step-mother who sends her two step-children, a brother and sister, out

into the world to fend for themselves or perish. They find shelter in a hovel which they share with three pigs which belong to the sister. Her brother sells the pigs in exchange for three dogs whose names are *Fios* (Knowledge) *Luath* (Swift) and *Tron* (Weighty). The sister is enraged and allies herself with a giant. Fios tells his master of the danger which awaits him; how the giant and his sister have set a poisonous dart above the door to kill him. Luath runs in first, and saves his master, but in so doing loses his tail. Then all three dogs upset a cauldron of boiling water over the giant, who is hiding in a hole in the floor, and he is killed – the only loss being Luath's tail! The brother goes to live with a beautiful lady in a fine dwelling and, after a time, returns to visit his sister, armed with three magic apples. The sister sets three wild boars on him but he escapes by throwing the apples behind him and hinders their pursuit by running through moors, woods and lakes, in which apple trees miraculously appear. But still they follow, until the three dogs manage to kill them. The brother persuades his sister to come with him and be a serving maid to the lady with whom he lives. Then the sister, consumed with evil jealousy, places a poisonous thorn in the bed and her brother appears to be dead – so after three days he is buried. But Fios tells Luath and Tron what to do and they scrape up their master and remove the thorn. He comes alive again, and goes home to his lady, where he orders a fire of grey oak to be lit in which he burns his sister to death.

A great many prose tales involve giants and the heroes of the legends, and their exploits in battle against the invading Norwegians; also boats, adventures underground, and an island with fire (probably Iceland). There are legends with 'ships fastened with silver chains and kings holding them', and of swords, spears and helmets with magical powers. An old horseshoe was a potent spell against the powers of evil and can still be found on most stable doors. Smiths were associated with gods. Vulcan was a smith; Thor wielded a hammer; even Fionn had a hammer to strike the Bell in emergency or for rejoicing which was heard in Lochlann according to a story in Barra.

Within the lore and legends many things were magical and sacred because of their rarity, and iron weapons were scarce. Over the centuries, mysterious virtues have been attributed to iron, and while stone and bronze weapons are common in British tombs, iron is rarely found. If iron weapons had supernatural virtues ascribed to them when iron was rare and when the quality was new enough to excite wonder, then other iron objects should have virtues, and magic should be transferred to new inventions. Iron swords were worshipped in Sythian times and human sacrifice made to them, and they were found in kings' tombs. A gun was fired over the back of a sick cow to cure it, or was used to break spells. Saint Dunston took the fiend by the nose with a pair of tongs. The fiend of popular tales is brother to the Gruagach and Glashan, once a skin-clad savage and the god of a savage race. Is it possible that this superstition is perpetuated by the retention of these metal objects scattered all over the island?

Horses were sacred and birds were sooth-sayers; apples, oak trees, wells and swine were magical. The touch of cold steel could break all spells. It shines – it cries out – and the lives of men are bound up in it, so perhaps the mystic sword may have been a god amongst the Celts. 'The white sword of light' of the West Highlands shone so that the giant's red-haired servant could use it as a torch when he drew water at night; it could have been of rare bright steel when most swords were of bronze, unless it was older

still and was a mythological flash of lightning. Giants always had swords and iron clubs.

Numerous mountains in all parts of Scotland bear Ossianic names and there are hundreds of places where these legendary exploits happened which can be identified. In the Islands and the West of Scotland, men appear to have been the reciters and tellers of tales, whereas in the East, where the heroics of the Finne were rarer, women for the most part were the narrators, telling of ghosts, apparitions, fairies and witches.

The hero of a story who had promised to give his soul to the devil in exchange for a great favour, asked his friends to carry out a grizzly deed. 'When I am dead open my breast and extract my heart. Transfix it onto a long pole in a public place and if Satan is to have my soul he will come as a black raven and carry it off; but if my soul is to be saved it will be carried off by a white dove.'

His friends faithfully obeyed his instructions. Out of the East came a large black raven with great fleet-ness, while a white dove flew from the West with equal velocity. The raven made a furious dash at the heart but missed, while at the same instant the dove swooped and carried off the heart in its beak, to the tumultuous applause of the spectators.

Men of extraordinary size feature largely in the ancient tales and legends. They appear as fearsome and terrifying beings or 'gentle' giants, invariably looking for trouble, and generally fighting or wres-tling without weapons. Brute force and cunning were their trade but sometimes they fought with clubs, as

did Hercules and many others. Giants were strange and their dealings with men often proved disastrous – as with David and Goliath. They seem to have had a sharp sense of smell, or perhaps being exceptionally large men they had huge appetites, as they usually ate their captives.

Giants were not all savages, and although many seem to have lived in caves, a great number had castles and large houses with hoards of treasure and spoil. Very occasionally a giant performed an outstanding feat, one of which is recorded as having happened on Barra. This giant fished up the hero of the story, boat and all, and threw them over his head. Giants seemed to know a little magic – which didn't always work, as they were almost always beaten by the courage and resourcefulness of smaller men.

Fairy folk were the opposite. 'Little people' may well have existed, as the Picts are thought to have been tiny and so are Lapplanders. Superstition has it that 'they', 'the little people', could be conquered by Christian symbols and were probably pagans. They may therefore have been living when Christianity was introduced.

It was believed that they had control over beasts, and were good to people who treated them well and punished those who did not. A squad of 'little people' could clean, spin, repair and do prodigious tasks during the night and so placate the wrath of a 'giant'. An offering of milk was thought to be a good means of propitiating 'the little people' and securing their good offices, thereby protecting the cows, herds and children.

BRISGEIN

Mil fo thalamh
Brisgein earraich.
Mil is annlan
Omhan samhraidh.
Mil is conail
Curral foghair.
Mil is cnamhsachd
Cnothan geamhraidh
Eadar Féill Andrais
    Agus Nollaig.

SILVERWEED

Honey under ground
Silverweed of spring.
Honey and condiment
Whisked whey of summer.
Honey and fruitage
Carrot of autumn.
Honey and crunching
Nuts of winter
Between Feast of Andrew
    And Christmastide.

The Weaver's Castle

Little is known of the weaver except that he was banished for some misdemeanour to the Stack Island to the south of Eriskay, which was a common enough punishment in those days. Viewed from Eoligarry across the white cockle strands and the translucent blues of the shallows, the islet rises abruptly from the sea, as its name implies. The weaver took a small boat and various implements of cultivation necessary for his survival. Realising that the task ahead would be beyond his own strength, he slipped across to Eriskay and helped himself to a fine white pony. Carrying a sack on his own back and with the assistance of panniers on the pony he proceeded to gather stones from the shore and carry them up the path to the top of the cliff, where he built himself a small fortified 'castle' and a dwelling place. It must have taken him many long months of arduous toil, living on fish, fowl and what he could grow on the island. When supplies ran out he went ashore and helped himself, as raiding was a common occurrence in olden days. Finally the white pony died of exhaustion, and the last two panniers of stones it was carrying remain as cairns at the top of the Stack and were probably left for use in defence. In his extremity it is doubtful if the weaver enjoyed the magnificent view to the north and south, up and down the Minch and over Barra Sound and out to the Atlantic, but the Stack certainly commanded an excellent view of the many ships which anchored in the Sound in the lee of the small isles of Hellisay and Gighay, which was useful knowledge to a man in such straits.

But first, he needed the help and company of a wife and he knew the very girl, who also had a little experience as a weaveress; so he set off in the month of July for a certain sheiling near Loch Eynort in South Uist. It was customary in the summer months for the crofters to go to the hills with cattle, milking the cows and calves, and the young wives and daughters acting as dairymaids made the butter and cheese for the winter. There was the usual happy gathering of young people and the weaver quickly spotted the girl of his choice. Making an instant decision he carried the girl – possibly a willing victim – off to his little boat. Over the years that followed she bore him four sons and proved to be an adept pupil in the art of raiding, wrecking and plundering!

Sailing ships at that time were mainly secured to their anchors by means of ropes; and when the wind was right it was an easy matter to slip out under cover of darkness and cut the hawsers of any boat taking shelter. Very soon the unfortunate ship would find itself drifting on to the hostile rocks of the Stack, where the weaver and his wife would be waiting to plunder the wreck. As their boys grew to manhood the wrecking reached an unacceptable level and an order was dispatched to destroy or apprehend the band. An armed cutter was fitted out for this purpose and while cruising near to the Isle of Gighay it spotted the weaver fishing with three of his sons. As soon as the weaver saw the cutter they rowed with all speed towards the Isle of Eriskay in the hope of finding a hiding place, but their efforts were in vain as the cutter was close behind them. They were caught on the beach and the captain slew all four with his sword and ordered that the blood be allowed to dry upon it as proof of the deed accomplished. Eventually, news of the killing circulated through the islands and the weaver's father-in-law rescued his daughter and his one remaining grandson, returning with them to South Uist. The castle has been empty ever since. It is said that the youngest son swore revenge and years later traced the captain of the cutter. When he boarded the vessel in Dunvegan harbour he found a blood-stained sword and slew the captain on the spot.

Calum Glic

One day in April some of the young Barramen were cutting kelp from the sea and carrying it to safety beyond the reach of the high tide. From there it was carried in creels by the girls to the machair. This heavy work was lightened by youth and laughing banter and as the day wore on others appeared to help and join in the fun. One young mother brought her baby and to keep him from harm wrapped him in a blanket and laid him in a wooden tub used for holding whelks, cockles and other shellfish. Time passed and suddenly the girl and her companions realised that it was almost dark and the tide coming in rapidly. With all speed she ran to where the child had been left in the tub, but to her horror there was no trace of either. Distractedly they ran about looking and shouting but to no avail. At the height of the panic one young lad ran for help to *Calum Glic* (Wise Calum) who was a taciturn man with uncanny insight, although he could be eloquent enough if the occasion arose. He went without a word to the shore and demanded exact information about the wind, the tide and when the tub was last seen.

Calum appeared to go into a trance – the second sight. He stared at the stars muttering to himself and trying to read the riddle of the tides. Round to the east of the island, in the channel separating it from the neighbouring land, was a rare phenomenon – contending tides. There, twice daily, the tide from the Minch and the tide from the Atlantic rushed to meet each other at the speed of a fast river. They met with wild turbulence in mid-channel at a point known locally as *Caol-an-Fhuaim* (The Channel of the Noisy Waters). The tub with the baby in it would be moved gently by the south-west wind that had been blowing, until it was caught in the swift currents from the Minch – after which nothing could save it. The wind had changed but that was scant consolation. Calum was quite calm as he came out of his trance, then he shouted with authority, 'Put out the big boat'. Willing hands rushed to do his bidding. '*Athainne*!' (A torch!) he commanded, and someone brought a glowing peat from the fire. Some also fetched unkindled peats which were put into the boat. Four young men went to the oars while the others held glowing peats to the wind, which gave a good halo of light on the waters around the boat.

'Steer on the blue star to the south of east', commanded Calum, and for an hour they pulled in silence, right out over the dark and stormy waters of the Minch. As one peat burned out another was lit from it, but the wind was increasing. 'Dip them in the sea', ordered Calum. 'They will last a little longer.' He was keenly scanning the water, his eyes, though old, seeming to cut into the darkness. Suddenly he shouted '*Togsuas an t-anthainne!*' (Lift up the torch!). The last glowing ember of the one remaining peat was held aloft, and there was the cockle-tub with the newly-awakened baby, smoothly riding the waves. Great was the marvel and the joy of it. Wise Calum removed his bonnet from his white head and reverently thanked his Maker for the guidance.

An old man told a story of how he was wrecked on an isle far away from Barra. He entered a house and was astonished to find that the interior resembled his own dwelling, and when a woman appeared he recognised her as his sister who had mysteriously disappeared years before. She treated him kindly and although he was somewhat unwilling to stay in what he knew to be a '*trows*' or 'fairyman's' house, he hoped his sister would shield him from evil. A little later a seal passed right in front of him and entered the best room, returning a few minutes later in the form of a happy, well-dressed man, who gave him a warm welcome. At supper they ate delicious cod and the '*trow*' eagerly told how it was caught. 'This morning,' he said 'I saw it to the north of Berneray and as he was good eating I had a mind to have him. But he was a great swimmer and I had an hour's hard chase before I caught him. When I rose to the surface, I saw the island before me and made for home.'

The Isleman in whom goodness is stronger than love, finding a Sealwoman bathing in the creek, will let her return to her natural element: but if love is stronger, he cunningly hides her skin and weds her on the third night after he finds her.

The Sealwoman, hot and tired baking the bread and making the churn against her husband's return from the hunting hill cried 'Ochone! the burning of me, what would I not give for a dive or a dip into the beauteous coolness of the cool sea‑water!' On the very heels of her words, who rushed in but her wee laddie, his two eyes aglow. 'Oh mother, mother, is not this the strange thing I have found in the old barley kist, a thing softer than mist to my touch!' And when she looked, this strange thing softer than mist, was it not her own skin! Quickly, deftly the Sealwoman put it on and taking the straight track to the shore it was nought for her then but a dip down and a keek up, all evening long in the beauteous coolness of the cool sea‑water. 'Wee laddie of my heart,' said she, 'when thou and thy father will be in want, set thy net off this rock and thy mother will throw into it the choice fish that will make a laddie grow and a man pleased with himself.' And the Sealwoman, with a dip down and a keek up, went on lilting her sea‑joy in the cool sea‑water.

Early one morning a young man spied a lovely girl sitting on a stone, singing very sweetly as she combed her long yellow hair. The lower part of her body was in the water, but he crept up quietly and put his arms round her. She looked round at him and it was love at first sight. They often met after that and she brought him jewels of many kinds, gold and silver with precious stones. Neighbours wondered how the youth had suddenly become so very rich. He began to ask his mermaid lover for more and more of the riches she said she found among the wrecks at sea. The diamonds – some of which were of immense value – he gave to other girls and in flirting with them he sometimes forgot his tryst with the mermaid, who became jealous, and upbraided him for his faithlessness in giving her presents to her rivals. After several quarrels she arrived one day in a beautiful boat, in which she offered to convey him to a cave nearby at Cliat, where she kept all the treasure ever lost. The prospect of such wealth was too much for him and they both sailed away for the wonderful cave. Soon after he got into it he fell asleep and how long he slept he knew not, but when he awoke he found himself secured by golden chains which allowed him to walk from the innermost recess of the cave, where large diamonds lay in a heap, to the mouth, across which was a seaweed-covered log. There he has been confined ever since, and his mermaid lover continues to take good care that he does not escape.

Long ago the islanders had a lurking belief in the truth hidden in the tales and legends; they were shy, proud and sensitive to ridicule and did not want to be laughed at by people of wider education. The story went that an old shoemaker had a tooth which he consulted as an oracle on all important occasions. He had only to touch it and whatever he required to know was instantly revealed to him! When one roams the islands it is well to remember that 'The Swan is the daughter of the twelve moons, the Seals are the Children of the King of Lochlann under spells, and the Mallard is under the Virgin's protection, and therefore all three are sacred'.

Much of the Hebridean poetry is about the Christ and the Virgin Mary, the Saints and the Blessings, the Isles of Song, the Labour, the Love and the music of the harp. There is an old saying in the Gaelic . . . 'Beautiful her music on the harp, more beautiful than her music, her goodness,' and the songs of the Hebrides have been immortalised for the greater joy of the world. The Gaels expressed their love, joy, drudgery and pain, with exquisite sadness through their music. Encompassing everything were the moods of the sea. The Singing Water, Sea Widow-hood, Sea-Longing, Fey Sea-Laughter, and the Rune to the Sea-God, Lear.

The islanders regarded the sea as a dark, cruel power, frequently wayward and generous but disturbing the mind with its awful mystery. Tales of the supernatural were told with an assurance which demanded acceptance, and local headlands, creeks and hills were endowed with their own legends. The sea was also a protection against enemies such as the Norsemen, those daring Vikings of exceptional seamanship who plundered and sought glory in strange lands. The islanders with their harsh environment, were cautious and less adventurous. Their legendary heroes, trusting in the dirk, their faith in the Almighty, and little else, went forward like the surge of the sea to embrace the challenge of life and death.

One wonders if the old way of life has been improved upon by modern 'progress' which, although alleviating some human misery, has also created a poverty of the spirit. Is it purely nostalgia to regard the past as a satisfying and worthwhile way to live?

Man can best find his God by going to the open places where great truths are often simple things. Barra stands, the spiritual home of her scattered people, her ancient rocks a symbol of eternal values.

A' GHRIAN

O Iain Mac Nill, coitear, Buaile nam Bodach, Barraidh

Fàilte ort féin, a ghrian nan tràth,
  'S tu siubhal ard nan speur;
Do cheumaibh treun air sgéith nan ard,
  'S tu màthair àigh nan reul.

Thu laighe sìos an cuan na dìth
  Gun diobhail is gun sgàth;
Thu 'g éirigh suas air stuagh na sìth,
  Mar rìoghainn òg fo bhlàth.